THE AMERICAN ENTERPRISE PARTY

(DRAIN THE SWAMP, REIGN IN BIG BROTHER AND THE BROTHERHOOD)

VOLUME I

THE AMERICAN ENTERPRISE PARTY

Volume I

The Swing Vote to Drain the Swamp and Reign in Big Brother and the Brotherhood

"This book is a must-read for anyone regardless of political preference or perspective, who might be contemplating political and economic change for the nation."

- Batya Weinbaum, The US Review of Books

"One other unspoken message coming through these pages loud and clear, is Jerry Rhoads' deep love of America. He obviously cares enough about his country to think deeply about its sad state and come up with some potential solutions."

- Dan MacIntosh, Pacific Book Review

JERRY RHOADS
Founder and CEO

Copyright © 2024 by Jerry Rhoads

All rights reserved. This book or any portion thereof may not be reproduced or transmitted in any form or manner, electronic or mechanical, including photocopying, recording, or by any information storage or retrieval system, without the express written permission of the copyright owner except for the use of brief quotations in a book review or other noncommercial uses permitted by copyright law.

Printed in the United States of America
ISBN:
    Softcover   979-8-9910186-9-2
    eBook

Published by: Rhoads Publishing
Publication Date: 06/25/2024

PREFACE

AMERICANISM MISSION STATEMENT

In America we now have two tribes fighting each other and losing the American Dream. The Left and the Right forgo the middle American voter, for one party control. A THIRD-PARTY SWING VOTE that breaks ties, does cost benefit analysis for accountability, and keeps the money-tics and partisan politics honest in operating the Great America Enterprise profitably. Using generally accepted accounting principles GAAP for reporting the financial condition of the Republic. By being the referee for consensus cost via benefit decisions making to avoid one-party control and bankruptcy. In God we trust, when Monetary Capitalists share and Human Socialists care, and where free market enterprise is truly laissez-faire.

THAT'S WHAT MAKES AMERICA ENTERPRISE GREAT,

WITH THE CHALLENGE OF GLOBAL TRADE.

WE NEED PEACEFUL COEXISTENCE DETENE TO,

KEEP AMERICAN ENTERPRISE RETURN ON OUR COLLATERAL GREAT.

PEACE THROUGH STRENGTH IS A STRONG ECONOMIC BASE (COST OF SALES AND OVERHEAD), ROI, CASH FLOW, AND NON-PROLIFERATION OF NUCLEAR WEAPONS OF MASS DESTRUCTION.

"We the people expect all American citizens to ask not, what you can do for your party. Ask what you can do for your own American Dream."

WHAT THE STATUTE OF LIBERTY REPRESENTS

(Not Blinded by the Light of the Benjamin Might)

Americanism the process of American monetary capitalism merged with American Socialism produces laissez-faire market enterprise, profits, capital, ROI, and cash flow. Financed by our system of laissez-faire competitive, color-blind economics. Human capital, the skills, knowledge, and experience invested in laissez-faire enterprise drives collective wealth.

$E=mc^2$ ... Enterprise = monetary capital times human capital squared = profit, cash flow, ROI in GDP, and GNP. Economics = cost of sales and budgetary spending and deficits = +/- spendable surplus for research and development that drives national growth and prosperity.

What do the scales of Lady Justice represent?

The balance (scales) represents weighing facts, and evidence to decide a verdict. It also shows her duty to restore balance to society. Although many people think of Lady Justice as wearing a blindfold, she can also be shown without one. Both versions highlight her impartiality. The rule of law prevents the law of rulers and regulators.

BLINDED BY THE BENJIMAN'S MIGHT. Ask not what you can do for your party. Ask what you can do for your country.   THE AMERICAN ENTERPRISE PARTY TRILOGY

AMERICANISM AND HUMANISM ARE THE AMERICAN DREAM

VOLUME ONE: THE MISSION OF AMERICANISM

VOLUME TWO: THE QUASI-REORGANIZATION OF DEBT AND DEFICITS

VOLUME THREE: RESTORE AMERICAN WORK ETHIC WITH HUMANISM

The America Dream's American Enterprise Rhoads theorem $E=mc^2$

Laissez-faire enterprise equals American Monetary capital times Human capital squared.
AMERICANISM = American Capitalism gestated by American Socialism multiplies prosperity to be shared by the shareholders, human capital, and stakeholders.
The Ten Tenets of Laissez-fair enterprise.
This formula works daily in all American businesses, small, medium, and large international enterprises.

Tenets of American Laissez-Faire Enterprise:

It's a world of competitive global forces attacking our values and internally woke reasons for changing our way of life. It's a war of doubt and fear won with faith and leadership standing up for the 10 tenets of American laissez-faire. Then the American Dream tenets of the Many are one result of each American striving for a quality of life.

1) Reward received is determined by the amount of risk taken. Protected by US bankruptcy laws and the rule of law.

2) The law of supply and demand for measuring markets.

3) Sharing is based on the skill to bill and the risk taken to produce goods and services creating GDP and GNP.

4) Earning is based on risk taken by learning a skill to bill for goods and services. Profits.

5) Competition creates optimal quality, innovation, and cash flow from GDP/GNP creating retained earnings for capital growth and reinvestment.

6) Quality creates cost savings and profits. Profits create growth. And capital for R&D and market expansion.

7) GAAP reports actual financial and operational results. Stock and bond markets report derivatives.

8) USA Debt clock and financial analytics are based on GAAP, a guideline for collective prosperity based on the cost of sales, profits, and cash flow.

9) USA balance sheet, sustainability is a current ratio of two times current assets and current debt, including accruals for future obligations, less than 85% of GDP and GNP.

10) Accountability for the above 9 tenets is the bottom line for measuring leadership. It's cashflow rewarding shareholders, funding workers for profit sharing, stakeholders for benevolent, and capital growth. Where shareholders share and stakeholders receive donations, not profits.

American Enterprise is not Woke capitalism or socialism. It's a free-market enterprise Capitalism (money) managed by Socialism (workers) for the prosperity of its investors practicing the above 10 tenets. Nor is there a need for a FREE-MARKET enterprise to practice or use the ESG index (environmental – social – governance) for evaluating Governance. That is done by www.usdebtclock.org, www.nationaldebtclock.org GDP, GNP, GAAP, and the WORLD global marketplace.

Supported by keeping the dollar as the reference currency as asset based in global trade exchange rates based on the power of the USA collateral reported by the www.usdebtclock.org
:

Precious metal reserves	$ 1,221,800,000,000
Mineral reserves	$ 5,701,800,000,000
Real Estate	$75,344,400,000,000
Land	$24,502,000,000,000
Stock Market	$50,908,000,000,000
Recaptured assets	$ 7,537,000,000,000
New energy	$ 3,970,000,000,000
Total USA collateral	$169,187,000,000,000
Per citizen	$503,700

Increasing at a trillion per month based on $E=mc^2$.

This dwarfs the old gold standard for debt and deficit backing. The problem is liquidity, and the American Enterprise Party proposes additional capital, not using taxation but Trade War Bonds to support the Volume Two of the Trilogy proposal for a quasi-reorganization of the debt and deficits using GAAP accounting principles and financial statements utilized to move Federal Reserve banking into the US Treasury department and using central banking and crypto our dollar currency for global trade exchange rates.

Finally, the underlying is rebranding America as Americanism based on humanism, replacing all the other isms. Americrats, Meritocracy, Ameritics as the branding for the voters to have a voice in what makes America Great, nothing else. The rest is how to Keep America Great. Ask not what you can do for your party. Ask what you can do for your country to Keep it Great. This is the capital and society working together as a laissez-faire enterprise, to protect a three-party debatable point of view for the constitutional and judicial secure vote to protect our financial and social standing as the United States of America leading peaceful coexistence in a volatile world.

VOLUME ONE

SAVE THE GREAT AMERICAN ENTERPRISE

The American Enterprise Party and its Platform (Drain the swamp and dispose of the alligators) What to Do!

Table of Contents

INTRODUCTION	1
THE GREAT AMERICAN ENTERPRISE IS BROKEN!	13
WHO IS WINNING THE GLOBAL ENTERPRISE WAR?	22
OUR BINARY TWO-PARTY ESTABLISHMENT POLITICAL SYSTEM HAS FAILED US	57
WHY AMERICA NEEDS AN EFFECTIVE THIRD POLITICAL PARTY AS A SWING VOTE	75
DRAIN THE SWAMP DISPOSE OF THE ALLIGATORS	96
THE AMERICAN ENTERPRISE PARTY PLATFORM	112
AUTHOR'S BIO	154

Introduction

In Volume One of the American Enterprise Party Trilogy, I write about what to do ... "Give me Enterprise or Give me Debt" a takeoff of Patrick Henry's famous statement "Give me liberty or give me death". A working subtitle of "Give me Liquidity or Give me Debt" proposes in Chapter 11 under the U.S. debtor bankruptcy code and Chapter 15 of the international bankruptcy law, a take-back of the value of the dollar by refinancing America into an equity-driven economy to save the American Enterprise from bankruptcy. By reorganizing our debt-based economy into an equity-driven Enterprise, as it was in the beginning, we emerge debt-free. With additional capital raised by issuing Trade War Bonds through the Department of Treasury.

For now, as monetized politics and debt are the focus of our regulatory nightmare with more and more infringement and new entitlements taking over the work ethic, we no longer work for ourselves; we work for the Orwellian Animal Farm (Oligarch) run by 545 politicians (100 Senators, 435 Congressmen, 9 Supreme Court Justices and 1 President, with the Red and the Blue parties fighting over power not solving budget deficits nor leading us to protect our honor in the world ... while China is breathing down our neck with a ten-year plan to overtake and destroy our American Dream.

After looking at the comparative analytics that follow, it dawned on me that America is back sliding and China is colliding with its human rights, an internal conflict between enterprise and communism, that is proving that Marxism and capitalism cannot be bedfellows. So, the CCP and the USA both need to realize that freedom and opportunity will be the winners and it is a matter of economics, politics, and trade not military and political strength that will win out. It is where monetary capital and human capital work in sync to form the perfect union of marriage called free market enterprise. The Great American Enterprise is being attacked by the existing binary two-party political system.

This is pitting businesses against government and needs the American Enterprise Party to control the sanctity of the American

Dream and defeat all the other isms with humanism ... the right to life, liberty, and freedom to pursue our individual dreams with equity, and equal opportunity for the greater good of America the Bountiful.

Therefore, in 1984, after rereading Orwell's book 1984, and continually checking out the Chamber of Commerce and Federal Reserve Debt Clock in New York City www.usdebtclock.org I began thinking about and writing about a viable third-party alternative based on the principles of Enterprise; representing the freedom of peaceful coexistence, with life, liberty and the pursuit of happiness for all Americans. Replacing all the isms with humanism (the synthesis of investment capital and human capital working together every day in the American enterprises) replacing the economic theory that capitalism and socialism are arch enemies and neither is considered the framework for the American constitution when in fact they are the foundation for living with humanism as the American Dream.

But it takes a true democracy to accomplish this marriage. Otherwise, as in the binary two-party political system that is gridlocked so it is in fact a mono party, we don't have a true democracy ... it's an oligarchy. The only way to return to the Adam Smith's vision of capital and free market enterprise for the people is to return to the constitution and the form of debate that accomplishes the American Dream. The problem is by its nature those who produce the wealth must share it with all. However, if you spread wealth (capital) too thin it soon disappears due to the lack of incentive to accomplish that dream. This dichotomy causes a struggle over who shall share in the wealth and for how much. This is where the dynamic of work ethic and patriotism weigh in. The law of diminishing returns applies ... "Those who work for the betterment of wealth shall share in it".

Also, a rereading of the 1932 classic "A Brave New World " in 2542 by Aldous Huxley where the "Bojanowski Process", decants babies produced from perfect embryo eggs into perfectly formed adults. This was to replace the current world with 96% perfect human beings where only one grew before, for populating the Brave New World. It was John Caliban, the Savage Boy selected to bless the technology for application to his uncivilized tribal community to prove its ethnicity, who rebels against the perfection of human embryos and threatens to expose the effect on his personal relationship with Linda and is driven to suicide

His demise results in the collapse of the futuristic technology of the Brave New World and sends a message that humans are sacred because of their differences.

I get the feeling that under the guise of technology we Americans are being drugged into thinking we can control life with genetics and cure systemic racism using brain washing by our social and news media to control the political narrative. Such movements of the 1619 project, critical race theory, Black Lives Matter protests, the green new deal, unfettered voting, with new entitlements reverse our freedoms to embrace zeitgeist (extreme socialism), the new progressive utopia. Hence, the extreme progressives, using counter culture woke propaganda (lies repeated till they become true) alleging a xenophobia mindset for identity politics making race the catalyst for creating a Brave New America rather than to improve and perfect our constitutional democracy model for the rest of the world.

Thereby, volume One justifies creating the American Enterprise Party Platform to propose solutions not debate issues between the oxymoron establishment two-party system we have evolved into. We don't have a democracy with a binary 50/50 gridlocked Congress. Not only is this an anomaly it is an intentional distraction used by the gang of 545 (100 senators, 435 congressmen, 9 supreme court justices and 1 President essentially an oligarch and politburo) as a control device to avoid true debate of national and local problems (labelled as issues by the politicians) and deprive us of effective bipartisan leadership.

As a result, we have disparities of Washington schemes and socialist dreams. And we are leaving behind the majority of Americans that aren't racists nor xenophobic. Ironically, the meaning of woke for America is reverse racism and should be denounced as propaganda and brain washing by Big Brother government, Big Sister Media, Big tech Brotherhood. The only redeeming factor is voting rights based on signature ID and not allowing harvesting of minority votes. The fact that identity politics is a power grab by one or the other parties lends itself to an effective third party representing enterprising Americans with an agenda of inclusion of diverse people and opinions who work for a living with family values and behavior rules that are cultivated by a school of choice education system run by families not unions. Any other agenda will pull us apart and result in conflicting views and sorrowful results. We finally are realizing we can't fight discrimination with reverse racism. And peaceful protests, regardless of the intent, turn into escalated riots that detract from any solution at all.

Then the BLM movement is demanding defunding of the police and doing away with enforcement to warrantless policing with prosecutors turning a blind eye to bail and indictment, immediately leading to enormous increases in crime and death rates. Especially in the minority communities where gangs prevail without restraint. Maybe the solution is to focus "Green New Deal" money into rehabilitating the ghettos and minority neighborhoods by rebuilding that infrastructure for enticing new small businesses and improving the schools and their dropout rates. Replace the BLM claims that 30,000 gangs in our cities suffer from injustice systemic racism with employment to rebuild their neighborhood. This lowers the poverty rate, increases graduation rates, reduces teen pregnancies and stops the development of criminals. By taking pride in a peaceful neighborhood with ownership in a small enterprise they are a part of the solution to the disparity in opportunities and take part in the American Dream. That is the America we all want … that's why millions are coming to our borders and end up falling short due to the misapplication of America's wealth.

This is the reason we need the American Enterprise Party that stands for Enterprising Americans workers who defend our country, believe in a greater power, freedom of speech and choice of work, feelings of security in our homes and communities, patriotic to the history and work ethics of the past, willing to take a risk to better their life and country, respect our flag, history and icons of the past, responsible for quality behavior values passed to their children, expect a government that will be accountable for its fiscal affairs and a believer in American democracy, the Republic, our constitution and foreign policies. To this end those who contribute to our America's prosperity shall share in that end. A member in the American Enterprise Party dedicated to a balanced Congress, Presidency and Supreme Court. So, help us God.

Of course, the George Floyd matter was a hate crime and the criminal has been prosecuted under the Rule of Law as are all other injustices be they black, brown, yellow, red or white. So, the fringe movements that form around anarchy must not be condoned by the media or the news or revolutionaries, left and right. If so, they are a part of the problem not an issue to be tabled and forgotten by Pollyanna politicians and pundits who are avoiding true solutions.

This approach is not just populous but more inclined to reduce the size of our institutions and upsize the influence of our human capital (social responsibilities) who pay all the bills in the long run and need equal and equitable representation. The majority of Americans are not practicing "Jim Crow" white supremacy divisions but are for "John Crow" black inclusion to avoid reverse discrimination under the 15th amendment and reverse bigotry among minority groups who support inclusion as the solution.

The bottom line for future competitive elections is we need new blood, not spilled blood, to bring new ideas and ideologies into play with a philosophy that for the greater good we need to teach our citizens how to fish not just give out fish with a hope that they will learn to be self-dependent. The 2020 Pandemic is proving that the use of fear as an agenda dilutes our independence and puts us at bigger risks than the virus itself. It will take a decade to wash away the impact that too much "town hall" and "speech writer" government has shaken us into new forms of communication, work and socialization that hopefully will he positive ... not negative with the continued use of fear to misguide us when we have the next worldwide epidemic turned into a pandemic.

In Volume Two the American Enterprise Manifesto, I write about how to do it after being told an effective third party will never happen because money-tics will prevail ... but like socialism everything is wonderful until we run out of the other people's money. So, it is about draining the swamp and timing is everything; the time has come to balance the books and the power. With the progressives taking over building back bigger government they will finally regulate the Great American Enterprise to its everlasting death. Unless the binary system of government is turned upside down. The meat of how to make sure a third party is viable there are thirteen ways (chapters) using the swing vote, we reign in Big Brother and the Brotherhood, drain the swamp, dispose of the woke alligators and why it will work.

USA War on Debt, China's Cold Warfare Chapter (1) Marxism, Avoid 1984 (2) Capitalism Embraces Socialism (3) Value of the Dollar, Fiat Money, World Pecking Order (4) Health Care for All, Save Medicare (5) USA Enterprise is Lassez-Faire (6) Humanism and Peaceful Coexistence (7) Honor the Flag and Our Leaders (8) Leadership, American Creed and Patriotism (9) American Enterprise

Economics (10) Quasi Reorganization of the Institutions (11) American Enterprise Politics (12) American Enterprise Party Platform (13)

The bottom line for volume Two is how we drain the swamp, kill the woke alligators and win the war on debt then deal with China and other threats by reigning in Big Brother and the Brotherhood Congress.

This limits Federal authority by decentralizing power to the States, promotes humane progress based on the constitution, defending the flag, protecting our artifacts and pursuing the American Dream culture that provides freedom and opportunity for all its citizens in a healthy, safe and financially secure environment.

(See Exhibit E Volume Two for eliciting your opinion on what is a problem versus just an issue to be tabled with a call for reform; a classic political stall tactic so the voters forget how that problem was squelched or perverted into a law with regulations that take away more of our freedoms).

In Volume Three of the American Enterprise Party Books, I write about who will do it ... we must restore worker patriotism that has been destroyed by apathy and how to ... "Restore the American Work Ethic" ... "Where oh Where has it Gone." It focuses on improving our output by revamping our input of human capital values. Work for the sake of patriotic pride and the quality of life not just for the sake of money and job security. As for my work ethic I have owned small businesses for 37 years, that I have started from scratch, creating jobs, and envisioning better management systems and methods for principally health care facilities. I have never been unemployed, never drew unemployment or worker's comp and have missed no time from my employment in 59 years.

I have either been extremely lucky or an image of my father a Great common, every day, blue collar, enterprising American who worked in the Firestone Factory in Des Moines, Iowa for 32 years. And even today I remember accompanying my father to union meetings and being influenced as a factory worker myself when I was employed by Firestone one summer. Those images were and are the foundation of the work ethic we seem to have lost and the scenario I propose as the solution to the demise of the American work ethic a victim of the new entitlements under the guise of fake news, identity news media, political propaganda, brain washing by social media ... we need ethical behavior for the love of all called Humanism for the four R's ... Reject Reverse Racism Restore Civility with Love:

CIVILITY

Webster defines civility as civilized conduct (especially: courtesy or politeness) or a polite act or expression.

Be it diplomacy
Or politically correct
Or being civil
Or being uncivil

Civility is not just being politically correct

Then why do we continue
To reduce everything to an issue
If it's a festering problem in the way
And our leaders dilute it to a foray

Inequality results in uncivil laws
Uncivil rights
When we humans let relationships
Be decided by Government

Equality only starts with civil rights
Without uncivil laws
Intruding on the relationships
Required to love thy neighbor

By living the 10 standards of behavior

Thou shall not kill
Thou shall not commit adultery
Thou shall not steal
Thou shall not bear false witness
Thou shall not covet your neighbors wife
Thou shall not covet your neighbors goods
Honor your mother and father
Worship the Lord our God

Thou shall not take the Lord's name in vain
Keep the Sabbath day holy

These 10 standards cross all lines
Of race
religion
geography
gender
and politics

From sea to shining sea
Freedom isn't free but a necessary decree

If God were President
I would more clearly see
Kneeling before the throne of dignity
But for the sake of my goal

And the feeling of civility and vision
It's saving my soul with humanism

    As the author of the American Enterprise Party Platform, I'm a product of a small farm community in Iowa that was called God's Little Acre in the 1940's as a totally dry town that even frowned on smoking and most certainly did not condone teen pregnancy or divorces. We had no minorities of color or religion . . . we were all poor to almost poor red neck white trash by today's standards. But out of that culture grew a common sense and hard work ethic. My dad for example was never unemployed never drew unemployment, never missed work at Firestone Tire & Rubber but went on strike every union contract year, for months on end, to make sure they protected their promised benefits that they never got.

    He, at the age of eighteen, and his two brothers had to leave the farm in 1929 during the Great depression when there were no grain for crops and no food for the 8 children, to ride the rails across America . . . his stories about working for a $1 per day with a noon meal, sleeping in hobo camps along the way, drinking moonshine for survival, jumping onto the railroad cars and surviving the trip for three years, then returning to the farm when they heard that the depression was over ..

. all of these adventures were featured in a recent HBO documentary about the Great Depression of 1929. Making him the man he was . . . a man of work that never swore or drank in his family's presence, never wanted any management responsibility and never missed work . . . the Iowa work ethic of old. I learned much from him that makes me What and Who I am today and much that I reject as well, including pure socialist, liberal, or Libertarian principles. Is this just conservatism with a different twist . . . no that is not my intent. . . I want more freedom to choose yes, but within the structure of Government of the people, for the people, by the people, not just by me or for me but because of me.

My father once said Firestone management was stupid because they paid union wages for piece work then had their ignorant production control retime the jobs so we made half as much as we used to . . . then we only worked half a day and still made our quotas. He, later on, was promoted to the end of the quality control line, checking steel belted tires for defects. It was when production managers decided to lower the quality standards to reduce the waste and defective tires were pushed through and Firestone was destroyed by lawsuits when the defective tires blew out and Bridgestone, a Japanese company, acquired them. After thirty-four years Dad retired at the age of 64 and sat in his chair for his final 18 years drawing social security and no pension, finally dying in a nursing home at the age of 82.

So, being an entrepreneur in America and a small business owner myself why would I venture into the buzz saw of conventional wisdom dominated by political pundits who intellectually spout "issues" as facts and facts as "no problems" as the domain of the establishment "Big Brotherhood" Congress, Big Media, the Big Tech, Big Box companies, Big Pharma, Big Unions and never putting forth the voice of the silent majority? Because CNN, Fox News, MSNBC, conservative radio, liberal leanings of the celebrities and universities are not reporting the depth or breadth of America's decline.

They are in fact the beneficiary of the hard-working enterprising majority who do not have a voice. I, as an unknown, nonintellectual, will be accused of being unqualified politically, negative on America and idealistic on foreign affairs. (Ironically the same rap Donald Trump got when he decided to run for and became the President). Right up front I want to state that America, in my view, is the greatest example of Capital (financial and human) driven Enterprise ever known to man and woman . . . including the British Empire, the past German and current Chinese versions.

However, all good things come to an end unless there is revitalization of the principles that got us here. So, much of this book is based on factual data and statistics gleaned over a number of years as I wrote manuscripts regarding the need for political and Government reform to ensure we worship Enterprise rather than institutionalized money. In my research I found that certain individuals have contributed to contrasting opinions that became movements and did solve social and economic problems. Why because they were first of all superior leaders and second dedicated to preserving the honor of our past generations and conserving the future.

Margaret Thatcher and Ronald Reagan were two such leaders of conservatism that inspired me to write this book proposing that we restore old American style Enterprise that evolved out of the slave supported plantations and Aquarian farm communities into the cities of industrial blue-collar workers and profit seeking white collar business owners serving our academic universities and institutions. But now such academic laws and Ph.D. regulators are stifling our effectiveness to utilize what we learn from the Universities and Colleges without allowing the private sector to manage the implementation.

Because of this infringement of Big Institutional Government (Big Brother) on individual creativity and freedom, for the sake of control by the Bigger Box stores, Bigger Pharma, Bigger Technology media and Bigger Universities and Institutions (the Brotherhood), economically called a "Monopsony", (sp ... means market controlled by the buyer of last resort ... government) we are hampered by our own incompetence because of a lack of competition and quality as defined by free market enterprise. To alter this **"Rome is Burning"** mentality we have to have a balance of the Private Sector and Public Institutions or we will evolve into a world of continued declining initiative and more divorces of thought, marriages and families.

UNCIVIL RIGHTS

Civil rights are the foundation
Of our democracy

And our standards
For human value

Uncivil rights are the foundation
Of demagoguery.
And the violations
Of human value

Be it a racial problem
Religious problem
Gender problem
Or a political problem

Then why do we continue
To reduce these to an issue
My point is that this deviates
Our approach from our personal interests

Not focusing on the interests
Of those who are the subjects
While turned to objects
By reducing civil rights

To uncivil rights
This is the "gimme" factor
In the equation of equality
And inequality

Equality it seems to me
Is what you can gain not what you're given
Regardless of circumstances
Or obstacles in the way

And inequality it seems to me
Is what you can lose not what you deserve
Because of the "gimme" circumstances
And wanting it just your way

Just another cry out for peace and tranquility
That's civil rights and civility

As we are born free not equal
And die equally dead with no sequel

It is opportunity that
Is being free to choose our own reality
When freedom and opportunity are the gradient
And effort is the quotient of what's real
Equality and the right to be free the intent

Gives all people liberty to be equal

The Great American Enterprise is Broken!
What to Do to fix it?

Is America an institution or an enterprise, an Oligarch or a Democracy? Or a Biden-Sanders-Pelosi-Schumer version of Castro's Cuba or Maderno of Venezuela? Or political sectarianism headed for authoritarianism or ideologically polarized by a wokeism culture war or all of the above ... whatever it is we are wasting away our Great American Enterprise fighting each other for control when peaceful coexistence acknowledges that it is humanism we desire. Only in a true democracy will debt and deficits be avoided and the market place dictates our economy ... while socialism commits to spreading the wealth and it disappears. How can you divide it equally and multiply it equitably? Equity meaning what we individually learn and earn.

In the book, the case is made for America being the greatest free market capital driven enterprise ever invented by humans, of humans, for humans. If you feel it is or not, why would we want to be controlled by a Few consisting of Big Brother Government, Big Brotherhood Business ... Big Tech, Big Box, Big Pharma, Big Corporations and Big Media using their corrupt economy to control the Many. So, our current financial and social problems need to be dealt with if we are to protect the American Dream. From this point on I will propose that America is the Great American Enterprise and how a third-party representation affects all of us. It's our enterprise that makes us great not our monolithic economy based on debt and deficit spending.

Adam Smith, father of capital deployment and Enterprise: *"The general industry of society never can exceed what the capital of the society can employ. Debt capital employed by society can be a friend to the needy and an archenemy of the republic."*

With a viable third party we pull votes from the Right and the Left extremes and do the Right Thing … serve the greater good for the majority of our citizens. With each party eventually having a third of the electorate there is no swing vote power over the other and the need for the filibuster is moot. Democracy in our Republic is then saved from "Bigger is Better" where the progressive intellectuals run our businesses into a Marxist institution, not for the enterprising American's individual common good.

Dennis Prager, a political pundit and educator, rightly says "the more government intrudes in people lives, the less important people feel, unless they work for the government. Yet to progressives the government should be involved in almost everything in people's lives. However, at a massive price: the more one relies on government the more one inevitably lacks a sense of importance in their lives".

Just ask yourself, as a voter, who would you pick a "better Red than dead pragmatic Republican" or a "Blue blood bleeding-heart phlegmatic Democrat" … or an "enterprising market driven American Enterprise Party Humanitarian" that wants every American citizen to be successful and healthy in pursing the American Utopian Dream. With an accountable government, fiscally, physically and socially, that promotes peaceful coexistence rather than cancelling our patriotic history and culture.

THE WHITE HOUSE

1600 Pennsylvania Avenue winds
As the sun shines
Towards the seat of power
A mortal spirit tower

Citizens support this throne
With votes alone
Hoping for humble leadership
With a just whip

Government is said to be in balance
Allegiance is the stance
Jeopardized by outside threats
Testing honor it begets

Branches there mostly theory
Much more than democracy
Its men asked to be more than self
With feelings on the shelf

President or Senator merely (wo)men
Born to die as we have been
But asked to assume our fate
By laws for land and State

Whether it be a white house
Or the shack in Foust
Men have declared their independence
To live free of immoral suspense

Could it be this right is abused
As to be heard is defused
By officials in secret chambers
Hidden from us voting members

Plato said of the price of freedom
That all want some
Regardless of the rational need
Dogs will even demand to breed

Orwell too predicted times of doom
As minds astute must loom
Squelching the simplicity of man
Until revolutionaries stand

Rome then Germany wrote the history
Of government by misery
Later we've read the immoral accounts
Of tactics we now renounce but pronounce

But have we learned our lesson
Or is man prone to treason
To principles based on declared right
With dollars wilting logic's might

No it appears people must weaken
To power of a rhetorical beacon
Aligning themselves to jobs and money
Ignoring goals of our country

So the White House up on Capitol Hill
Crumbles to a weakened will
By men's weakness to assert and compromise
Themselves to intellectual lies

As Polonius warned through Shakespeare
Yourself you must fear
For truth unto other self must be
Before life is honesty

To thine self be true or history will be you

Will this wrong ever be righted
Before our destiny is kited
So the majority is represented
And the power of money has been repented

Elections and selections
Fair and square of insurrections
Must be based on principles
With political partisans feigning disciples

While freedom and equality if any
Representing the Many
Defending the invincible crew
Against the dominant Few

While the White House and ACLU must defend you

Evidently, with our new Democratic leadership America has no debt limit, with $30 trillion in recorded debt, and $158 trillion in unrecorded obligations creating a credit rating of, at best B-. What next? More trillions spent on progressive infrastructure dreams. What do we do when we can't cut checks for social security, Medicare and Medicaid claims, government payroll and interest payments to China, Japan and trillions of dollars of 10-year treasury notes with interest due and past due? Since American enterprise is insolvent, as debt escalates, the value of the dollar shrinks and cash flow disappears, America needs a third political party to act as the legislative "swing vote" on saving the Great American Enterprise from bankruptcy and ensuring our global sovereignty.

Is the USA doomed by its own creation … aka too many laws, regulations and regulatory agencies, using misleading institutional budgetary accounting, with debt and deficits created by a two-party political system based on woke philosophies, by bigger is better government, corrupt media and failing small businesses?

When you think about it, the recent China Virus Pandemic was mismanaged by Fauci "Fear Factor Quack Science" using the principles of Political Science. It's Big Brother and the Brotherhood consisting of Big Tech, Big Box, Big Media, Big Pharma, Big Unions (all government employees especially teachers) all deemed essential while the rest of the businesses were closed down … all for the progressive's desire to Dump Trump at any cost to society.

Whereas, decentralized, solving of these problems, led by those who believe in the American Dream is better for the greater good. Giving rise to the very movement we need which is an effective third political party to bring down Big Brother government and the Brotherhood by draining the swamp of its woke alligators.

(See the following Big Brother's swamp financial data based on (GAAP) generally accepted accounting principles, reported on the debt clock for second-by-second financial condition of the troubled American government and economy: www.usdebtclock.org).

1. **Negative net assets**, using GAAP generally accepted accounting principles, means zero financial net worth when national assets of $161 trillion are less than the total national debt of $210 trillion.

2. **Negative cash flow** $10 trillion in expenditures and $7 trillion in receipts every year creating accumulated deficits of $158 trillion based on generally accepted accounting principles.

3. **Negative debt limit** of $27 trillion suspended during the 2020 election is exceeded by $3 trillion with the credit rating declining.

4. **Negative net revenue** (current tax revenues are only half of budget outlays). Unfunded Federal, State and Local Government pensions approach $900 billion.

5. **Negative borrowing** strength due to current insolvency and borrowing more for funding the Pandemic stimulus, Infrastructure and the Green New Deal. With 30% of the national debt being held by our advisories, USA is subservient to its own ambivalence.

6. **Negative future** with the new progressive administration increasing taxes, rushing into additional debt financing of social programs and proposing with HR-1Federalizing a voting consortium of unregistered voters, packing the Supreme Court, elimination of the filibuster and electoral college that unfettered will keep one party in control without opposition. The Oligarch is then formed and freedoms are doomed.

   To prevent this the American Enterprise Party will represent the Swing Vote that only takes one seat (example Joe Manchon D West Virginia) in the 50/50 Senate and the narrow margin (with the Squad demanding a radical agenda) in the House to make a difference in correcting the financial and social problems. That a gridlocked no consensus Congress with a 88% voter disapproval rating and a progressive President have dealt to its 200 million enterprising American workers and their families who need fair and equal representation as the people's third party. The American Enterprise Party www.americanenterprisepoliticalparty.org,

7. **Positive Solutions the USA** must strengthen its position in the world economic (enterprise) war by realistic GAAP reporting of its fiscal and physical condition and refocusing its reorganization plan to pay down debt and strengthen its economic offensive by realizing we have vulnerable opponents. The focus on collaborating our capital resources and human capital to include an effective third political party that exemplifies the power of the American people. Per **Ronald Reagan**: "Above all, we must realize that no arsenal, or arsenals of the world, is so formidable as the will and moral courage of free men and women. It is a weapon our adversaries in today's world do not have."

   Our ammunition is American Enterprise that brings monetary capital and human capital together every day in American business to form a coalition of bedfellows not enemies. It takes capital to fund business and humans to manage those resources (assets, profits and cash flow) that are generated by this dynamic duo. Therefore, the need for the American Enterprise Party to fend off the extremes of the two-party establishment system and become **the swing vote** in arbitrating the divergence of the conservative and liberal, Red and Blue, left and right progressive philosophies and policies that are destroying the Great

American Enterprise. Make American Solvent Again. MASA … true liberty for all comes at a cost and profit.

With a viable third party we pull votes from the Right and the Left and do the Right Thing … to serve the greater good for the majority of our citizens. This is where populism is replaced by Humanism for populating Capitalism with diversity seeking opportunity for all to fulfill an obligation to pursue peaceful coexistence around the world. But this must be done rationally and financially sound considering the implications:

INFLATION DEFLATION STAGNATION

(Simple economics is never simple it's an imposing dimple
So, keep it simple Simon or suffer an infested pimple)

Inflation
(paying more and getting less)
I see it when I pass the gas station
I see it when I get my spendable ration
I see it when I read about the nation

More Inflation
(getting less and wanting less)
I can't view it with elation
Nor can I understand its creation
But I'm suffering from its impregnation

More Inflation
(An expectant economy's indigestion)
A declining dollar chasing frustration
And government's spending sensation
In the name of a political indigestion

Less Inflation
Maybe it's just a result of my faulty expectation
That my welfare check comes before excess taxation
And my personal acts don't contribute to stagnation

A pregnant economy due to excess consumption

And not managing the business gestation
With a buying and borrowing obsession

Which means it's our personal responsibility to budget
Our costs and debt for maximum profits and return on investment
So, the government doesn't increase taxes on what we used to earn

Deflation

(A pregnant economy due to excess consumption
And not managing the business gestation
With a buying and borrowing obsession)

Which means it's our personal responsibility to manage
Our enterprise and affairs for maximum return
So, government doesn't destroy initiative
Just for what we used to earn

Growth was good

Nation was strong

Profits were earned

now

Government can't save us

Dollar value is down

Plunging us into endless debt

Deflation is primarily due to the Federal Reserve monetary policies
And interference with member bank discount rates sinking the
subprime markets and the value of the dollar

Stagnation

(spending less and getting less quality)

Is when the government gives away too much
Controls lives with a tax crunch
Telling everyone what they should eat at lunch
And runs everything on an academic hunch

Is when debt service becomes an excessive burden
On the cost of producing products and services for a profit
And the government jobs make GDP grow
Even though it adds nothing to cash flow

Inflation deflation stagnation

*(The imminent demise of a nation
Is time for a reorganization)*

Elect someone with a business reputation
Where the Capitalist is the beast
The Socialist is the least
The Worker is the yeast
The Consumer is the feast
Then it's time for a third party
The American enterprise Party
The swing vote party that pulls

The two-party extremes towards the middle
And lets the lassi faire market decide the ride
By bringing together the Capital and Worker

For liberty and opportunity for all to decide
To Drain the Swamp and dispose of the alligators

TO SAVE THE AMERICAN DREAM

Who is Winning the Global Enterprise War?
(USA Oligarchy versus CCP Autocracy?)

USA Oligarchy: United States of America a system of constitutional government where 545 people (100 Senators, 435 Congressmen, 9 Supreme Court Justices and a President ... the only positions with a term limit) having control of the Federal and State governance, including enterprise and its institutions. **No longer a democracy due to the lack of term limits and a gridlocked Congress. Also termed a monopsony, the purchaser of last resort with an economy of excessive spending. Virtually a political cartel run by government. Ultimately, Big Brother and the Brotherhood a corrupt oligarchy.**

CCP Autocracy: China Communist Party has a system of autocratic government by one person (Xi Jinping) and a politburo with absolute power over its people and all governmental affairs. The government is the capitalist and the people are subservient to the Motherland. CCP is intent on defeating the USA for its prominence in worldwide trade, standard of living of the Few and strength of its military using Wolf Warrior as their mascot for the CCP cold war on USA.

GLOBAL ENTERPRISE WAR SCOREBOARD

In the finals, the USA the defender of a capital driven free market enterprise is leading but fending off a CCP Monopsony control of its enterprise aligned with oligarch monopolies. Who is winning?

Who are the finalists in the first international Globalization Enterprise War? Of course, it's USA and CCP who lord over Japan,

Russia, India, South Korea, Mexico, Canada, Israel, Arab Emeries in Division One, North Korea, South Korea, Britain, France, Italy, Iran in Division Two and everyone else in Division Three. Of course, America says they are in front with China second and the rest fill out the bracket in division one. What's the debt clock (www.usdebtclock.org) and public information available on Google regarding CCP's business practices, to enable us to score the playoff between USA and CCP in the first Global Enterprise War finals?

	USA V. **CCP**	
	Oligarch	**Autocrat**
Population	330 million	1.411 billion
Employed workers	169 million	775 million
Elderly over 65 (77 million Boomers)	46 million	145 million
GDP	$21.6 trillion	$14.8 trillion
Federal Debt	$28 trillion	$ 7.0 trillion
State and Local debt	$3.3 trillion	not applicable
Federal Debt to GDP	129.92%	45% GDP
Federal, local and State spending	$10.1 trillion	$ 5.3 trillion
Federal income tax revenue	$ 3.4 trillion (39+%) Biden policy	$2.8 trill.(3 to 45%)
State/local value added tax revenue	$ 3.6 trillion	$4.2 trillion
Unfunded govt pension liability	$ 7.3 trillion	$5 trillion funded
Property tax	$546 billion	None
Tariff tax revenue	$75.4 billion	$-75.4 billion
Trade imbalance	$-917 billion	+$311.1 trillion

	USA	V.	**CCP**
Government employees	22 million		10 million
Government payroll and benefits	$1.9 trillion		$202 billion
Government pensions cost	$345 billion		$40 billion
Total recorded govt debt	$85.7 trillion		$8.1 trillion
Personal debt of citizens	$21.1 trillion		$1.1 trillion
Mortgage debt	$17.1 trillion		$4.3 trillion
Student load debt	$ 1.7 trillion		nonexistent
Credit card debt	$ 1.0 trillion		$2.5 trillion
Federal Reserve unfunded interest	$11.2 trillion		$258 billion
Central bank assets	$ 7.7 trillion		$3.3 trillion
Top 1% wealth	$63.1 trillion		4.5 millionaires
Bottom 50% wealth	$ 1.9 trillion		85% inequity
Total national assets	$160.9 trillion		$90.4 trillion
Social security liability (see table)	$ 21.2 trillion		$137.1 billion
Medicare liability	$ 32.7 trillion		private $10k per head
Unfunded Liabilities	$162.2 trillion		$728 billion
Net worth of the country	**$-1.3 trillion**		**$ 6.7 trillion**
Cost of Government	**$ 10.1 trillion**		**$ 1.3 trillion ***

*Chinese bonds for funding central government and infrastructure 10-year yields 3.22% are CCP costs of government (USA investor' bond holdings in China amount to $100s of billions).

	USA	**CCP (1)**
USA has negative net worth	$-1.3 trillion	$+6.7 trillion
USA has negative cash flow	$-3.2 trillion	$+6.7 trillion
USA has negative net assets	$-2.3 trillion	$+6.7 trillion
USA shipping costs for imbalance trade	$-1.9 trillion	$+1.9 trillion
USA score v. CCP score in Global War	$-4.2 trillion	$+8.6 trillion
CCP Current leader of the Global Enterprise War	$12.8 trillion	

Footnotes:

1. *CCP is the owner of the 70% of Chinese enterprises, and also is on cash basis of accounting with plans to convert to generally accepted accounting principles (GAAP) in near future.
2. *CCP controls major percentage of USA supply chains.
3. *CCP 775 million low paid workers in one government union, 149 million self-employed business owners and nearly 300 million migrant workers. USA 124 full time employed 26-million-part time, 12 million unemployed.
4. USA $10.1 trillion cost of running the USA enterprise, CCP $1.3 trillion.
5. USA $7.0 trillion in tax revenues, CCP $7.0 trillion value added tax.
6. USA $21.1 trillion in GDP. CCP $14.8 trillion GDP.
7. USA $162.2 unfunded liabilities, CCP $7.0 trillion, CCP $728 billion pension unfunded debt.
8. CCP $7.0 trillion bond debt 10Y yield 3.22 % rating AAA.
9. USA $85.7 trillion bond debt 10y yield 1.2646%, rating Aaa ($1.07 trillion held by CCP and $1.25 trillion by Japan).
10. USA defense spending $721.5 billion, CCP $183.8 billion military budget.

The share of public property in China's national wealth has declined from about 70 per cent in 1978 to about 30 per cent in 2015. More than 95 per cent of the housing stock is now owned by private households, as compared to about 50 per cent in 1978. Chinese corporations, however, are still predominantly publicly owned: close to 60 per cent of Chinese equities belong to the government. Also, threatening the CCP are 376 million Tui Dang believers who have opted out of the communist party professing their independence and beliefs. They expect to be 500 million by 2026 in a movement to change China's Marxist government.

To pacify its 775 million workers the CCP has a comprehensive social security system, where it's not enough that employers are simply willing to pay. Whenever hiring new staff, employers need to register them with the local Social Insurance Bureau and the Housing Fund Bureau to initiate or reactivate their corresponding accounts. Further, although both employer and employee are obligated to make contributions, it is generally the employer's responsibility to correctly calculate and withhold the payments for both parties. Meanwhile, employers are obliged to make timely payments for themselves and their employees. A late contribution can result in a fine, while failure to contribute may lead to onerous labor disputes. In case of severe and multiple violations, the company might be put on an HR "name and shame" list, which can do significant reputational damage and create barriers to future recruitment.

One thing to be noted is that the employer's obligation to make adequate and timely contributions cannot be alleviated or exempted by reaching a mutual agreement with employees. In practice, China's employers and employees (especially those whose gross salary is not high) may mutually agree not to contribute to the social security schemes or to make contributions on a smaller basis, to save labor costs and maximize the employee's take-home payment. However, the court would consider such an agreement to be invalid in the case of a labor dispute between the employer and employee. The employer might be required to repay the social security evaded or pay extra severance payment to its employee in case of termination.

(In America we call this (GAAP) generally accepted accounting principles for enterprise. In this book the author is proposing that

USA also needs to use GAAP in its financial reporting taxation and budgetary system).

China's Social Security System			
Category	Contribution*		Description
	Employer rates	Employee rates	
Pension insurance	Around 20%**	Around 8%	Designed to provide necessary
Unemployment insurance	0.5%-1%	Around 0.5%	In the event of redundancy, the employee may claim unemployment benefits for a maximum of 24 months.
Medical insurance	5%-12%	Around 2%	Designed to cover part of the employee's treatment cost in the event of illness or non-occupational injury
Work-related injury insurance	0.5%-2%		Designed to cover the cost of treatment should an occupational injury or illness occur
Maternity insurance	0.5%-1%		Designed to cover the female employee's medical expense of childbirth and their salary
Housing fund	5%-12%***	5%-12%***	Designed to ensure that workers save to purchase house

* The amount of contribution in each category is calculated by utilizing the employee's payment base figure and multiplying it by different percentages required by each local government entity.
** Pension insurance contributed by employer can be lowered down to 16 percent starting from May 1, 2019.
*** In certain cities, employer and employee are allowed to contribute more than 12 percent.

Graphic © Asia Briefing Ltd

Governmental accounting reform has been an important issue of China's Party Central Committee and State Council. From 2013 to now, China has successively promulgated several policy documents in all aspects related to the reform of government accounting. In 2013, a document named China's Party Central Committee solving Some Major Issues was about comprehensively deepening the reform. It proposed that the country's budget management system and government financial system were not perfect, especially the government's financial reporting. China should try its best to build an accrual accounting reporting system. **In 2014 the newly revised budget law also proposed that China needed to put accrual basis into government financial reporting. At the same year, the ministry of finance in China had established a comprehensive "accrual government financial reporting system reform plan", and the plan explicitly pointed out that making the government financial report comprehensive, fully reflect the government's financial position**

and operating results, must use the accrual basis of accounting principles (GAAP).

The USA Big Government Swamp financial condition: On the basis of GAAP, generally accepted accounting principles, USA is insolvent, with negative net worth, negative net assets, negative cash flow. Currently USA is on budgetary accounting with the modified institutional cash basis that is cooking the books for the reporting its financial condition. For any other enterprise USA would be considered insolvent and a candidate for reorganization under Chapter 10 of the bankruptcy code. It looks like China also realizes the failure of their accounting system and plan to make the change to GAAP. This puts them ahead of us unless we reorganize our financial affairs. USA is borrowing money to meet payroll of 22 million government employees, with an unfunded pension liability of $7.3 trillion, unfunded government social security plan of $1.2 trillion, unfunded government health insurance plan $1.5 trillion and unsustainable fixed overhead of (difference between tax revenues and budget expenditures) of $6.1 trillion.

Side bar: the author, as a CPA consultant to the State of Illinois headed up a project to convert the state to the accrual basis of accounting in 1977 that was supported by Illinois Governor Walker. After the presentation by Mr. Rhoads the governor decided that he wanted nothing to do with GAAP. When he realized the ramifications of reporting the State's finances on an accrual basis would show the state to be insolvent, he shelved the project. And to this day the State of Illinois doesn't report its financial disaster on the accrual basis of accounting ... as a result Illinois is third to only California and New York in cooking the books and misleading the voters on the deficit spending financial condition of the Republic.

News Release: What is the CCP comprehensive Plan to be the World's Leader? According to Chairman Xi Jinping "we want to defeat USA by influencing their world dominance in the UN, WHO, WTO, NATO, World Monetary Fund, Olympic Committee and World economic development". To accomplish this, he supports the five-step plan.

1. Steal USA technology and improve on it then sell it back to us.
2. Expand territory in South China Sea, Africa, South America.

3. Build global economic influence through trade agreements.
4. Influence worldwide institutions with their monetary resources.
5. Influence USA elections and leadership with hacking and propaganda.

To do this CCP plans to conduct political warfare on the USA by supporting identity political candidates, critical race theory, climate change, university trust funds, investment in USA treasuries and collaboration with USA enemies. Also, CCP, with its "Wolf Warrior" attack if attacked motto has its eye on taking Taiwan, Philippines and Hong Kong back into their fold to takeover semiconductor (computer chips) production, capital formation and banking in the South Seas. This dilutes USA's influence and puts our diplomacy strength in doubt according to the State Department.

Examples of their implementation of this plan … Per recent events, the CCP will subvert the USA in its Iranian nuclear deal. News release: China and Iran make a deal … Iran has a new benefactor … the CCP will buy their oil in malfeasance to the Paris Accord and USA sanctions on Iran's missile development. CCP has expanded their infrastructure investment in their economy and according to news reports, assisting 20 other countries by investing in the world's other emerging economies.

China now controls the electronics and semiconductor (chips) industry with its rare earth mining investments and its plan to take over Taiwan Semiconductor Manufacturing Company (TSMC) while the USA is funding over a billion dollars to have TSMC build a plant in Arizona. The winner of this battle must protect the sovereignty of Taiwan and Hong Kong through putting pressure on China's dependence on America's markets and its ability to support the supply lines now in place.

Powerful hegemon key electronic semiconductor chip producers, rare earth mining companies and 5 G telecommunication corporations related to national security must not be deployed outside the USA or our defecto enemy CCP will control our economic future. This becomes the basis of the new cold war.

CCP's pledge is to "love the motherland and the people are to study well, exercise well and be ready to contribute all their strength to the cause of communism for the defeat of the USA".

Even though China is not yet using GAAP, it is in their plans to do so, they are incurring less unrecorded liabilities. So, at this point USA is losing the Global Enterprise War, by the CCP score of $+8.6 trillion to a USA deficit of $-4.2 trillion per year with China winning by $12.8 trillion per year. Even worse, China with its cheap labor and using USA consumption markets for distribution at no cost. Also, China now controls supply lines of American business in pharmaceuticals, hard goods, clothing, electronic technology components manufactured in China, autos, most other products distributed by China through their use of USA franchises, to the tune of China's $14.8 trillion GDP per annum.

The shipping and express airline cost of transport of Alibaba and American companies' products overseas to USA @ 10% of CCP, GDP or $1.5 trillion shipping costs to America's distributors or assembler's, per annum. The purpose of this book is to resurrect the USA supply lines, shift manufacturing back to America, offset the imbalance of the accumulated trade deficit debt of $3 trillion against the cost of the CCP Pandemic calling the debt owed to China as a payment for the USA cost of shutdowns and deaths due to the Corona Virus apparently transmitted from the Wuhan laboratory.

Predictably CCP can win the Global Enterprise War outright by having lower labor costs, funded fringe benefits, lowest government overhead, lowest R&D costs, no union interference, nominal long-term debt, low shipping costs, low marketing, R&D and distribution costs, producing the highest profits per product line. With cash reserves ($3.5 trillion exchange reserves and gold bullion of 5,000 tons) for R&D (mostly stolen from USA) and infrastructure technology positioned to win the Global Enterprise War every year. But the USA is not out of the game … it has official exchange **reserve** assets held by the FED of about $514.41 billion **U.S.** dollars in 2019. At that time, the central bank of **the United States** held approximately 8,133.53 metric tons of gold. (As of December 2020, **the United States** had the largest gold reserve – more than 8,000 metric tons of gold. China at this time has about 5,000 metric tons of gold and is a primary buyer in the market).

On the other hand, China needs four things USA has:
1. Food production and distribution.
2. Energy production and distribution (natural gas and carbon-based oil).

3. Capital access to the NY stock and bond market.
4. Technology developed by the USA Military, Big Tech and Big Pharma.

While China plans, using "Wolf Warrior" diplomatic warfare to divide and conquer, USA implodes and is divided internally. The CCP sees themselves as a rising power versus the USA a fading dominant power called the Thucydides Trap (a collision of a rising power with a disparate power) and they are using China, Inc. (CCP) to recruit using their 1,000 Talents Program through espionage and talent attraction including every tactic of propaganda and brain washing on our social media. This includes capitalizing on the gridlocked Congress and a new Administration that tends to be passive on foreign affairs with their CCP 'friends'. The source being The Epoch Times, Google search, Wikipedia, and media outlets. This consists of the following CCP plan predictions:

1. Recruit talent worldwide that has access to technology for theft.
2. Purchase innovative companies and control all private companies in China such a Huawei, that operates internationally, using them for infiltration into stealing trade secrets and intellectual property.
3. Recruit or attract talent back to China from USA and downplay human rights abuses.
4. Takeover Internet, utilizing Facebook, Twitter, Google and broad band with fake accounts, using their version of social media pushing Communism as a religion.
5. Takeover Twain, Philippines and Hong Kong for technology.
6. Convert globalization to "Made in China by 2025".
7. Have the Yuan replace the dollar as the reference currency worldwide.
8. CCP money invested in Silicon Valley, USA universities and hacking Government data to get access to technology and get a political advantage with the following products or data breaches:
    a. Rocket engines and space travel.
    b. Sensors, chips (semi-conductors) and rare earth components.
    c. 3 D printers, solar panels, electric autos.
    d. Flexible screens.

e. Bio technology.
f. Artificial intelligence for block chain currency.
g. Military air surveillance with drones.
h. Space exploration and dominance of surveillance satellites
i. Hacking pipeline and electric grids, voting systems, GPS systems, biological health and census data.
j. Hacking stock and bond exchanges for raising capital to implement their plans.

It appears their vision is to create a revitalized cold war on democracy with Marxism, Socialism and eventually Communism as their end game. With Russia, North Korea, Iran and others standing in the wings ready to pursue a one world dystopia based on a campaign of fear as predicted by George Orwell's "dark age of unreason" in 1984. Example: the release of a Covid virus on the world from a lab in Wuhan and blame the USA for its origin. USA must become proactive to collectively defend our democracy with a synthesis of policies, capital and talent for defending our Great American Enterprise against this new technological cold war. To that end our leaders must be schooled in this threat and end the gridlock with patriotism paralleling that of World War II. Together we stand, politically gridlocked we fail. Looming below the surface of CCP's plans are the question of President Biden and his son Hunter's prior business involvement in Chinese, Russian, Ukraine and other foreign countries. Example: President Biden's ambivalence regarding the Russian pipeline after closing down the Keystone Pipeline in USA to make America Green and his ignorance about the energy independence movement started by President Trump. This blemish must be eliminated by the Congress on a bipartisan basis to prevent the problem of political "pay for play" implications with potential cold war enemies.

After this extensive analysis of America and CCP's competition it becomes obvious that USA needs a third political party representing 169 million enterprising Americans that merges capital formation and human capital into the American Enterprise Party to be the swing vote to bust the binary gridlock administered by the Red and the Blue no consensus political parties. No longer should we pit entrepreneurial capitalists against the activists for social justice. In an enterprise they work together as a public and private partnership successfully every day of the week by collaborating their purpose and successes for the common good.

The American Enterprise Party would propose, as an example of that partnership, being committed to restoring the current state of the American infrastructure; fiscal, physical and environmental. This would replace current Red and Blue proposals that don't focus on the true American infrastructure root problems using ear marks and allowing the Green New Deal socialist ideas to be financed. Following is an American enterprise solution not a political proposal to push progressive socialist programs.

1. Restore by reconstruction of inner-city slums, ghettos and crime centers. Treat the inner cities and small depressed communities as enterprise zones that need to hire the locals (including gang members) to redevelop their neighborhoods and small businesses for the economic good of our under privileged Americans. This strategy is to build on the work ethic and put it to work on the good of the country as well as eliminating the excuses of why we have crime in the cities … it's disgraceful to see how the underprivileged have to live and survive. A basic rule for human dignity is to have opportunity be the primary part of the solution.
2. Restore police departments to support reconstruction of the inner cities. During the George Floyd revolt against policing we need to balance reforming the enforcement of the law to reinforcement of the basics of being suspects treated like a human being and for the human being to act like one.
3. Restore the businesses destroyed during violent protests and riots.
4. Finance steps 1 thru 3 with public and private revenue bonds collateralized by Federal, State and Local governments.
5. Rehabilitate streets, highways, bridges, water processing systems, transportation.
6. Close borders by completing the deterrents (complete the Wall, support ICE law enforcement and deportation of illegals).
7. Restore the natural gas leases and restart the Keystone pipeline for bringing the national energy independence back into balance.
8. Defer or slow down the Green New Deal, with current move to electric transportation and energy conservation for bringing emissions and carbon into compliance with the Paris Accord. Accelerate conservation of farm lands and forests to bring carbons downward to the earth's habitat restorative powers.
9. Establish ongoing infrastructure funding as 5% of annual GDP and 5% to continue war on debt as an ongoing budgetary line item.

10. Bring troops home from Afghanistan where we have spent $2.4 trillion dollars and $1.9 trillion in Iraq. Estimated $6.4 trillion total spent in the Mideast conflicts. And focus the military on the reconstruction of our inner cities and deputize the 30,000 inner city gangs to be paid to help in this plan.
11. Amend the Constitution and pass term limits for Congress ... three terms in the house and two terms in the Senate. We need new blood in Congress as well as an effective third party.

The American Enterprise private public partnership would focus on reducing crime in the inner city by coordinating the employment by private contractors including neighborhood gang members, legal and illegal immigrants and local unions to fix the most pressing problem in America ... crime, guns, gangs and assisting the police departments to reduce escalation with community stop and search for cleaning up the squaller and underserved inner city services to a respectful level in jobs, education, social and medical services.

We must make the crime rate, policing, public and private education, inequities in income levels and inequality in entrepreneurial opportunities (Commit $500 billion to Enterprise and Opportunity Zones over the next decade) the number one priority in a Rebuild of our Inner City and underserved rural communities as the 2021to 2031 Infrastructure budget. We should label this as American's Enterprise commitment to peaceful coexistence of the races, religions, sexes and creeds for preserving and committing our resources to saving the American Dream.

Rather than spending $100 trillion on climate change with the Green New Deal socialist loan program. Instead take the money that has been dedicated to that approach by:

Bank of America	$445 billion
Goldman Sachs	$750 billion
Morgan Stanley	$750 billion
Citi Group	$1,000 trillion
J. P. Morgan	$2.500 trillion
Total commitment	$5.445 trillion

Because it will take public and private partnership to help finance the net zero transition around the world, while the earth manages itself at no cost if governments preserve natural resources (Kiss the Land, Netflix). Otherwise, as usual mankind will screwup the earth's natural habitat (Mother Nature and Father Time biorhythm and immune system) as the greenhouse effect is rendered useless the globe will overheat wasting resources:

Government backed enterprise loans	$95 thousand billion's
Total Green New Deal	$100 thousand billion's wasted in its intent

A thousand billion here and a thousand billion there is still insane financing … Jerry Rhoads

Should invest the $5.445 thousand billion's private investment in true infrastructure projects:

1. Restore and rehab the inner cities with enterprise zones.
2. Modernize smaller communities.
3. Fix public schools' curriculum and facilities.
4. Clean up the oceans and smog in cities with natural energy.
5. Replace the lead-based watering systems.
6. Restore habitat with conservation of the earth's farming for revival of the rain forests and natural growth of carbon dioxide absorbing plants which was proposed by the Paris Accord and is being implemented by the USA farming community.

Since China has a 10-year infrastructure plan already in motion that will put them ahead of America we must alter the progressives Green New Deal into an American Enterprise Opportunity Plan funded by public and private investment with improved GDP as its goal. Even though China isn't complying with the Paris Accord they are preparing for the next decade of competing for leadership in the World's pursuit of dominance. Therefore, we must focus on our fiscal and environmental infrastructure to abort that threat. In the meantime, Biden's Build Back Bigger is focused on progressive socialism not being fit for the economic war. So, it's not Build Back Better. It's Bogus. Our money will no longer be green nor will our environment be free of the benefits of private investment if we react to government fear factor not common-sense solutions. Those progressives who profess humanity can manage the earth by deprivation are wanting power not a cleaner house.

The intent of the founders and authors of the constitution planned that turnover in the Congress would bring new ideas for solving national problems not compromising issues. As they had theorized that two-party system has become inbred and ineffective.

While America Burns, the Congress Fiddles With "Issues" not "Problems" by Jerry Rhoads', podcast <u>Mar 23 2021</u> "The Great American Enterprise Manifesto" on Spotify.

Have you wondered, as I do, why everything in our culture is an "issue" not a "problem" to be solved? To me that means "no problem" just give me a tissue while I compromise the issue". I believe this is a strategic political tactic by the two-party system to avoid being held accountable for creating problems needing to be solved by the leadership of our country run by the gang (Oligarch) of 545 elected officials (100 senators, 435 congressmen, 9 supreme court justices and a President) that don't want to be challenged on our deep underlying financial and social problems. Just listen to the change in priorities when each of us say issue when we should be saying problem … the new and worst cancel culture word is dumbing down our values and beliefs. (See Exhibit F Volume II for more).

Rome, also an oligarchy, is the best example of a great empire society that consumed itself with power and control of its people's emotions and values. While the Senate debated issues (fiddled) and the military carried on with its intent to rule the world, Rome's problems were burning it internally. Without competent leadership, the issues overshadowed the internal problems, that would spark the fire of over consumption and over indulgence in a violent culture. Julius Ceaser, elected pontifex maximus (High Priest), allegedly by heavy bribes, profited from the use of mass media to entertain the people with gladiators, excess consumption of food, sex and addictions and land grabs.

The Senate was led by Consuls (Senators) who commanded the army, presided over the Senate and executed its decrees. Ceaser formed a political alliance with Pompey and Marcus Lincinius Crassus, the wealthiest man in Rome, who was elected lead Consul of the Senate. Ceaser's army successes and conquests aroused Pompey's jealousy leading to the collapse of their political alliance. As result, Ceaser was appointed Roman Consul and Dictator of the empire. But he was assassinated on March 15, 44 B.C. by a group of Senate conspirators who believed they could restore the Roman Republic. However, the "Ides of March" plunged Rome into civil wars destroying the Democratic Republic forever.

America, in many ways, is an exact replica of the rise and fall of Rome.

Our Ceaser is Donald Trump and our Pompey is Joe Biden and the Democratic Party. President Trump's successes and conquests aroused the Senate and House jealousy, leading to the political alliance of both parties during a Pandemic to eventually dump Trump. The "ides of March 2021 led to the revival of the Democratic party as the progressive movement to destroy America with excess spending and destruction of the free-market enterprise envied by the rest of the World. Why else would every refugee want to risk their lives to come to America? Better yet, why would we let them embed themselves without vetting their abilities, health and contribution to our economy and culture.

The deterrents to open borders, as enacted by President Trump have been flushed away by the Biden Administration using human rights as the reason. **Ironically this woke movement siting white Americans as imperialist and** racists in its application is reverse racism. When in fact the majority of Americans aren't racists nor Marxists or Fascists.

If America was this inept why else would China steal and pillage our technology as if it was their ideas, make it better then sell it back to us as second-rate quality? Sort of reminds me of our new President taking credit for rolling out vaccines as if he had solved the problem that President Trump had invented. Shame on him for being the typical "do nothing for 47 years" politician. Along with the quack scientist Dr. Fauci also wanting to take credit for something he hadn't accomplished in his 45 years in the bureaucracy. So goes the two party political system and institutionalized government.

With the new Administration led by Marcus Lincinius Biden, the newly elected President, all of the successes accomplished by Trump (Ceaser) were reversed by the progressives under the executive orders and policies written by Senators Sanders, Schumer and Nancy Pelosi Speaker of the House thus creating a Congress with a 12% approval rating, bent on destroying America's sovereignty and capitalist control. Using mass spending bills, trillions in stimulus money funded by a state of fear, conducted by 22 million bureaucrats using the "issue" campaign that ignores the problems it causes, possibly destroying the Republic forever.

All because we have two binary parties debating issues causing gridlock in Congress to distract enterprising Americans from the real problems of our financial collapse (see debt clock http://www.usdebtclock.org) ... thus the burning of America's future as our Rome's "ides of March" 2021 style. Financially, we are broke and the Republic is being destroyed by the media and big business. Our borders are broken, overwhelmed by immigrants that expect their share of this American Dream with our Machiavelli leaders welcoming them as the new Republic voters putting the Democrats in control as emperor Pro-Tem of the disappearing American Empire. The Chinese are taking advantage of this by embedding green card college students for later sabotaging American society. Also, CCP is making behind the scenes contribution totaling $400 million dollars in American higher education.

Using an incompetent President Marcus Biden in charge of the executive orders to bypass a gridlocked no consensus 50/50 Congress (Roman Senate) to promise open borders for all, free education for all, health care for all, equal pay for all, clean energy for all, blanket amnesty for all, HR1 voting rights for all, reparation for immigrants, child care tax credits and write-off college debt. Then funding bloated government with more taxes on the wealthiest (except for the mileage tax that hits the little guys the hardest), cuts in defense spending, cuts in free market entrepreneur's compensation, redistricting the electoral college, control of the capital driven stock market, enacting gun controls, overturning Roe V Wade, cutting entitlements for the elderly, expanding the Supreme Court and eliminating the filibuster. Destroying the Republic by adding new states (Washington D.C. Puerto Rico, Cuba, Virgin Islands) and the Democracy with unrestricted mail-in voting, embracing harvesting voters from the age of 16 on, including every person, in a more fearful but diverse population.

We then are a country of one-party issues not two-party problem solving. A country with defunding police, rewriting bail laws causing declining enforcement of the Rule of Law. A country of over population and millions unemployed (mostly illegal immigrants) living in tents cities or squalor in the inner cities. A country of fear and lock down for any virus, real or not real" conceived by the bureaucrats. A country that can't service its debt. A country ignoring the debt clock (www.usdebtclock.org) that is showing America as essentially bankrupt. A country of one-party rule with two Red and Blue factions that fiddle with gridlocked no consensus issues while Washington (Rome) Burns from incendiary financial and social problems.

To avoid becoming the next Rome, Russia, China, Venezuela, Cuba, Great Britain or Nazi Germany as another example of how a great empire (the United States of America) became a canceled culture. A new third party (the American Enterprise Party) will emerge and become the swing vote in the gridlocked no consensus Congress to implement problem solving and bring the left and right extremes towards the middle using peaceful coexistence for the greater good of its enterprising people; practicing humanism as a restored, rational, common-sense, patriotic culture.

Thus, saving the Great American Enterprise for the benefit of its enterprising American citizens and its constituencies, while not limiting the spread of the wealth to qualified legal immigrants who will speak our language, pay taxes, become citizens of the Great American Enterprise in pursuit of the American Dream so they don't later turn coat and lead the Asian revolution to unseat America as the world leader in commerce, technology and military.

To Prevent This We Must Return to Democratic Values:

Margaret Patcher (1925-2013) (Prime Minister of England 1979-1990)

- "There is no such thing as society: there are individual men and women, and there are families".
- "If you just set out to be liked, you would be prepared to compromise on anything at any time, and you would achieve nothing".
- "It is not the creation of wealth that is wrong, but the love of money for its own sake".

Margaret Patcher dealt with similar economic problems in England, that America now has, *as leader of the Conservative Party from 1975* to 1990 and Prime Minister from 1979 to 1990. She was an advocate of privatising state-owned industries and utilities, reforming trade unions, lowering taxes and reducing social expenditure across the board. Thatcher's policies succeeded in reducing inflation, but unemployment dramatically increased during her years in power. However, it was her leadership that directed the British away from socialism back to capitalizing on enterprising workers for the sake of the country's future.

The movie about the *Iron Lady* did not give justice to Margaret's influence in making one of the most significant socioeconomic changes of all time. Since she died in 2013, we are not going to have her council or involvement in world economics or enterprise so in America, in her memory, we must challenge Big Brother Government and the Socialist form of Democracy at all times. She and Ronald Reagan had a bond based on America's philosophy that the individual makes the country the country does not make the individual. It is such leaders we have to revere and not be deterred by spin doctors and lobbyists.

Ronald Reagan (1911-2004) (President of the United States 1981-1989)

- "Entrepreneurs and their small enterprises are responsible for almost all the economic growth in the United States".
- "Government exists to protect us from each other. Where government has gone beyond its limits is in deciding to protect us from ourselves".
- "Government does not solve problems; it subsidizes them".
- "Government's first duty is to protect the people, not run their lives".

Ronald Reagan on his eight-year watch was following a one term Democratic President in Jimmie Carter who pushed American businesses to the brink with his 23% Keynesian prime rate of interest to quell record inflation and destroyed the Savings and Loan business forever. President Reagan was lucky to inherit Alan Greenspan as the Chairman of the Federal Reserve Bank . . . who by chance had ultra conservative Libertarian leanings? President Reagan also engaged Dr. Arthur Laffer, Ph.D., who became the father of supply side economics, as his chief advisor on Taxation, who then, with a Republican House put trickledown economics into action. With the interest rates and monetary system in check and taxes being cut, small businesses were relieved of burgeoning debt and created products and profits at a record pace.

Unemployment declined, but still the State and Federal deficits rose. Unfortunately, Bush senior following Reagan, was a civil servant not Entrepreneurial who famously said "read my lips, no tax increases" then proceeded to increase taxes to his demise. Then Bill Clinton the smooth-talking salesman had the country in a developmental mode until the high-tech bubble burst in 1999. According to Allen Greenspan, his Fed Chairman, in his book "The Age of Turbulence", only Reagan, Clinton and Kennedy understood the monetary system and its role in promoting free market enterprise.

Later we were to find out that neither President Bush nor Chaney nor Paulsen had the "balls" to stop new Fed Chairman, Professor Bernanke from bursting the housing boom overnight causing the worst depression since 1929 to fulfill the book he wrote that proposed printing money to stop the member banks from closing while destroying $30 trillion dollars in American's home values. Then he and the Bush Administration blamed Wallstreet's subprime mortgage arbitrage rather than fessing up that it was a diabolical mistake. (See Volume Two Chapter Four "Pop Go's The Monetary Balloon" for what likely caused the depression of 2007).

All the while conservatives on the Republican side acquiesced to a staggering war budget and a fiscal depression under George W. Bush, selling out to a protectionist Government pursuing a One World version of Liberty. Regime change was the game headed up by his Vice President Richard Chaney using WOMB's and oil, in the Middle East, as his weapon.

Then Obama, a liberal constitutional professor and street attorney, rides in on his oratory ability, right in the middle of a depression and worsens it with a misguided $700 billion stimulus package for the bailout of large banks and big business, financed by the Federal Reserve Bank selling "T" Bills to China and imposes the Biggest Entitlement of all time . . . Obama Care that may well be the demise of the Great American Enterprise and its 77 million retiring, unhealthy baby boomers.

(Later President Trump, during his short term in office, also attained the magna cum laude for his handling of the Fed, keeping the exchange rate and inflation at near zero and the stock market at all-time highs of 30 thousand directly attributed to the tax cuts to corporate

America ... then after the 2020 election, the cuts were reversed by the Biden Administration by increasing rates to the wealthy and corporations, that may well cause price hicks and a deflated currency during an economy with unemployment, trying to recover from the shutdowns during the Pandemic. Already prices of essentials at the pump and grocery stores are up 20% and in the nonessential service industry as much as 50% .... As my poem predicted inflation produces deflation then stagnation.

I quote Ronald Reagan again: "Above all, we must realize that no arsenal, or arsenals of the world, is so formidable as the will and moral courage of free men and women. It is a weapon our adversaries in today's world do not have"

We need to realize that reality does not create us we create reality with common sense solutions to problems not just debating political issues. We can learn much from Margaret Thatcher and Ronald Reagan in their campaign to have "Government protect us not run our lives" as opposed to what Karl Marx stood for in his Communist Manifesto.

To Do This We Must Reject Marxist Values:

Karl Marx (1818 to 1883) author who wrote the Communist Manifesto in 1848 that puts forth his ten steps necessary to destroy Capitalism and a Free Enterprise system. Then replace it with a system of omnipotent government power, so as to affect a communist socialist state. Unfortunately, many Americans are being transformed into a Communist State of mind, by myths, fraud and deception under the color of progressive lawmakers and politicians; namely, extremist Republican and Democratic parties alike.

Karl Marx, in creating the Communist Manifesto, **designed the 10 planks AS A TEST** to determine whether a society is becoming socialist then communist or not. The 10 PLANKS stated in the Communist Manifesto and some of their American counterparts (in parentheses) are . . . Marxist theory that race rather than class to justify the Black Revolution with the socialist platform called the Black Lives Matter movement due to social and economic inequality will become a third party standing for race not caste or class using identity over substance. This will include defund police, promote the 1619 project, use critical race theory in their campaign, open borders, sanctuary states and cities, massive spending on infrastructure, climate change,

Green New Deal, Ear Marks, Welfare reform, limit military spending, counting on 18 to 20 million more voters to become the swing vote. Funding to be generated through the Big Box companies, Big Media, Hollywood fund raisers, Big Brotherhood Business. To prevent this from becoming a reality the American Enterprise Party will contest these moves with humanism and peaceful coexistence for all races, creeds, genders and religions. Following are the 10 planks and the status of them being implemented in America's government regulatory agencies and the free enterprise marketplace.

1. Abolition of private property and the application of all rents of land to public purposes. (Imminent domain lost to Federalism of property).
2. A heavy progressive or graduated income tax. (Graduated taxation on adjusted gross income and progressive taxation on corporations) (Biden's reversal of Trump tax reduction and proposing record tax increases).
3. Abolition of all rights of inheritance. (Biden resurrecting Inheritance or death tax).
4. Confiscation of the property of all emigrants and rebels. (Laws preventing aliens from owning property). (Biden limiting ICE deportation) (Biden opening borders to illegal immigrants promising equity and domain).
5. Centralization of credit in the hands of the state, by means of a national bank with State capital and an exclusive monopoly. (The Federal Reserve Bank and legislation, rules and regulations). (FDIC) (FEC).
6. Centralization of the means of communications and transportation in the hands of the State. (FCC) (FAA) (FHA) (FMC) (FTC).
7. Extension of factories and instruments of production owned by the state, the bringing into cultivation of waste lands, and the improvement of the soil generally in accordance with a common plan. (EPA) (Army Corp of Engineers) (FERC) (OERE) (NRC)
8. Equal liability of all to labor. Establishment of industrial armies, especially for agriculture. (NLRB and Unionization of labor). (EEOC) (CPSC) (ATF) (Department of Justice) (VA) (ETA).
9. Combination of agriculture with manufacturing industries, gradual abolition of the distinction between town and country, by a more equitable distribution of population over the country. (Corporate conglomerates with farm quotas and subsidies). (CFTC) (FCA) (FDA) ... Big Brother designation of Big Government, Big Box,

Big Media, Big Tech, Big Pharma as essential to saving America from financial destruction during the Pandemic and funding sanctuary States and cities promising housing and stimulus checks to illegal immigrants.
10. Private education for all children in public schools. Abolition of children's factory labor in its present form. Combination of education with industrial production. (Public education funded by property taxes, gambling taxes, sin taxes, Power Ball and Lotto). During 2020 Pandemic the takeover of education by Teachers Union and holding parents and children hostage for their own protection and purge for more funding by being nonessential.

The progressives (politicians) of the twenty-first century who seem to believe in the SOCIALISTIC and NEO-COMMUNIST concepts, especially those who pass more and more laws, rules and regulations implementing those ideas, are contradicting their oath of office and to the Constitution of the United States of America. "Johann Wolfgang Von Goethe" — 'None are more hopelessly enslaved than those who falsely believe they are free".

Peace on Earth Towards all Men and Women; Must Be USA's Reformation of a Democratic Society with Rule of Law and an Enterprising Work Ethic Culture becoming the World Leader as the Great American Enterprise. No longer can it be acceptable to acquiesce to radical extremism when America is becoming the nesting place for the world's refugees. The world needs to fix the problems we cannot fix and should not if we are financially bankrupt.

Open Borders' Cost, who will pay it?

The following projections are based on estimates made by accountants and economists.
$60 million per week to house and feed illegal immigrants.
$1.500 trillion per year $ 5 million per week to process and relocate illegals.
$300 billion per year $1 billion per week to enforce our current laws
$520 billion per year.

Total cost per year for open borders $2.32 trillion as our spending for 2020 exceeded income by $6.1 trillion and the deficit was funded by debt! Taxpayers aren't paying for the $6.2 trillion bills passed by the House ... deficit spending is dependent on the Federal Reserve to print currency or issue 10 or 30 year Treasuries. Secretary of the Treasury Yellon says her major concern was not the debt but the interest rate may increase and the interest payable may exceed cash and borrowing availability. She and Fed are considering issuing 100 year Treasuries to defer the interest problem. Of course we can owe more if we defer it to another century … that's doing something insane saying it will get better.

What are the other costs to our Republic?

1. The following are being embedded into our open boarders' and sanctuary country:
    a. Drug dealers from cartels in Mexico, Central and South America.
    b. Illegal immigrants and refugees from 48 different countries; many testing positive for Covid-19 and the rest represent super spreaders because of the congestion in housing and transportation. Dr. Fauci our resident scientist refused to respond to requests to stop the crisis with National Guard placed at the borders to prevent the spread of possibly a new stain to our American cities.
    c. Terrorists from Mideast and Asian countries.
    d. Human traffickers from third world countries.
    e. Spies from China and Russia infiltrating into our colleges and universities by funding scholarships and harvesting potential activists while stealing our technology.
    f. M-13 and Asian gang members who detract our police from enforcing current immigration laws.
    g. Homelessness and unemployed illegals in our inner cities and rural communities that don't have skills nor speak English. And have no known insurance coverage for Covid-19 and are dependent on public housing and health in numerous states.
2. Immigrants are competing for low paying jobs in a struggling economy for small and mid-size businesses. Currently we have 40 million immigrants with approximately 50% undocumented.
3. Consuming our welfare spending for food stamps, low-cost housing, free health care, leaving less for our needy citizens. All of this is being funded by an American debt financing splurge.
4. Ever increasing homelessness in sanctuary States and Cities. Biden administration housing the thousands in hotels in sanctuary cities at a cost of $83 million dollars per day.
5. Unrestrained population growth in our inner cities and rural farm communities.

6. Over load for our struggling policing and border security personnel.
7. Populating the illegal voting problems that exists in America.
8. Diluting the American Dream:
    a. Tax avoidance of illegals that is drainage of our debt financed welfare state.
    b. Export of cash to foreign nationals by illegals.
    c. Dilutes our national priorities for using public funds to educate, house and feed illegals with low skills and language differences.
    d. Opens our inner-city slums and small border town citizens to spread of Covid-19, crime, drugs and illegal human trafficking.
    e. Judicial system is overwhelmed and is not able to keep up with deportation of illegals as the Biden administration put a moratorium on such outcomes.

What impact does this have on our pending 2020 census numbers? With illegal undocumented immigrants now pouring in at a 6,000 per day who will account for them when it comes to voting or should I say illegal voting? Due to this problem, not an issue, the USA has added 10 million to our census since 2000. Without an accurate census, including illegals and undocumented immigrants, how can we manage our finances and control our runaway cost of housing, educating and treating them for health care problems, if we can't even account for our citizens, who are migrating away from the borders to sanctuary cities and states, who will also suffer from this disaster.

Who will be held responsible for the atrocities that are occurring at the borders of Texas, Arizona, New Mexico, California, Louisiana, Oklahoma, etc. It has to be the Biden administration that issued the "one come all" executive order that allowed those seeking refugee status, unattended children, Covid-19 cases, cartel traffickers, drug and M-13 gangs and death of those being promised sanctuary ... all undocumented and are allowed to relocate all over the country. This is resulting in a violation of our rule of law and our standards of human rights, thereby increasing our housing, education and health care costs for undocumented immigrants tenfold.

What is the solution:
1. Enforce current immigration and border laws. Then prosecute and deport offenders. Reinstate agreements with emigrating countries to slow the current onslaught.

2. Engage the source of the problem in the countries causing the exodus.
3. Restrict foreign aid to the countries causing the problems.
4. Complete the wall and enforce the security at the points of entry into our country.
5. Stop the flow of refugees and illegal immigrants with our national policies and priorities, particularly with the impact of an international Pandemic costing us our goal of herd immunity.
6. State governors are held responsible for enforcement of all of the above and maintaining a census of that category of our population, each year, for managing the costs. Their taxing body must keep track for the financial impact of immigration on an accrual basis of accounting for tracking the cost for budgeting and enforcement of taxation laws.
7. Governors should immediately use their authority and send the National Guard to the borders to stop the flow. As these illegals come to their state they are accepting the responsible for their welfare.
8. Repeal sanctuary city and state laws and withhold funding for such unamerican policies.
9. Media must accurately report the problem and solution to hold the politicians responsible for violation of the country's safety and security laws.
10. Elect third party candidates who want Americans protected first and foremost.
11. Set up analytics for holding each state governor accountable for securing our borders with reduction in illegals for the Greater Good. Then use incentives of Federal revenue sharing for those States that are successful in allowing legal immigration to work for America's benefit and preventing all of the above problems.
12. Impeach the sitting President for the atrocities and violation of existing immigration laws.

Summary:

We Americans are being held hostage by a binary two-party political system that is currently a 50/50 mono gridlocked Congress with ineffective leadership and patrician policies while arguing issues rather than enforcing our existing laws. The unmanageable financial and long-lasting societal cost are everlasting for our children and grandchildren due to the potential demise of the American Dream; such partisan executive orders used for the political reversal of policies that were working towards making America safe and secure must be exposed and stopped.

The time has come for America to have third-party intervention, as the swing vote, to break the gridlock and move towards fair and equal representation so all Americans matter.

Maybe, as **John Lennon (1940 to 1980) songwriter and singer**, advises us in his song "Give peace a chance", that we can lead the world away from the ism's to Peaceful coexistence. . . which is a quantum paradigm leap away from totalitarianism to self-determination with freedom to create a peaceful world using Humanism.

"Give Peace A Chance"

Ev'rybody's talking about
Bagism, Shagism, Dragism, Madism, Ragism, Tagism
This-ism, that-ism, is-m, is-m, is-m.

*(racism, fascism, socialism, communism, **humanism**)*
All we are saying is give peace a chance
All we are saying is give peace a chance
C'mon
Ev'rybody's talking about Ministers,
Sinisters, Banisters and canisters
Bishops and Fishops and Rabbis and Pop eyes,
And bye bye, bye byes.

All we are saying is give peace a chance.

THE PRINCIPLES OF HUMANISM

The golden rule "those with the gold shall rule" to be replaced by
"Those with common cents have the human votes to rule"
The rest are wokes spouting racism, socialism, capitalism, fascism,
ism, ism ism when all we want is humanism"

The complexities of our world
The battles for flags unfurled
Is there simplicity there
That can explain
How to have happiness in spite of pain

Is it so hard to know
Not why but how to grow
Does it have to be deciphered
By the professors of Harvard and Yale
Turning the glow of life
To a confused pale

Why does it have to be so hard
Why is it scientific to have grass in the yard
Or success dependent upon the turning of a card
Nay that's only the human's way
Wanting to impress
To assume the power
And control the press

Rather than giving a simple yes
We pull it through the cloak of complexity
Watering it down with ingenuity
Until there's no such thing as purity
No such thing as the ease of an understandable truth
And the uncast shadow of youth

That merely assumes that we have to live through monsoons
And shouldn't have to control the weather
Or recreate the aerobics of a feather
It's not necessary to multiply divide and carry

For the sake of making it hard
Till jokers are wild holding the hole card

With common sense and good will
Lost to the complexity of nonsense and hell
While the soothsayers spout
And the intellectuals pout
About
Politics climate change terrorists
And all other indefinable events

By referring everything to an algorithm
Or an Evangelical hymn
To make sure once again
That a Trump card doesn't win

The other cards in the deck
Dumbing down the electorate
Making transparency after they inspect
And keeping public opinion in check

With condescending words to deflect
"Now look"
"Free health care is a right"
"It's an Issue not a problem"
"Now Listen here"
"It's God's will"
"Right to life"
"Right to choose"
"Black lives matter'
"White lives matter more"
"Prayer out of the schools"
"Debate away the country's fate"
"Free college tuition"
"Unlimited minimum wage"
"Maximum wage"
"Public officials are above reproach"
"The President's irresponsible"
"It's the media's fault"
"Issues issues issues

While the ACLU says "let the flag burn and
There's no such thing as straight or fag,
him or her, yes mam no sir"

What happened to common everyday
Horse sense
Gambled away
On dollars and nonsense
Oh for the forties and fifties when a dollar was gold
And patriotism never grew old

Purchasing votes with good ole common cents
Instead of debt, bit coins and finger prints
Doing away with all those isms
With the principles of Humanism

Life liberty and the pursuit of opportunism

The following is quoted from a newspaper article published in the Orlando Sentinel,

Monday, August 8, 2011
Charley Reese's final column for the Orlando Sentinel

Who is the Oligrach of 545 vs. 330,000,000 People

(100 Senators, 435 Congressmen, 9 Supreme Court Justices and 1 President)

- Politicians are the only people in the world who create problems (and call them issues) and then campaign against them.
- Have you ever wondered, if both the Democrats and the Republicans are against deficits, WHY do we have deficits?
- Have you ever wondered, if all the politicians are against inflation and high taxes, WHY do we have inflation and high taxes?
- You and I don't propose a federal budget. The President does.
- You and I don't have the Constitutional authority to vote on appropriations. The House of Representatives does.
- You and I don't write the tax code, Congress does.

- You and I don't set fiscal policy, Congress does.
- You and I don't control monetary policy, the Federal Reserve Bank does.
- It is an establishment Oligarch… "a gang of 545 = 100 Senators, 435 Congressmen, One President, and 9 Supreme Court Justices. . . that equates to a 545 gang of human beings out of 330 million who are directly, legally, morally, and individually responsible for the domestic problems that plague this country. *Why then would we believe that they can solve them"? See complete article by journalist Charley Reese in chapter 10 Volume II American Enterprise Party.*

THE SENATE
By Jerry Rhoads

They sit behind
Dappled desks
On seats of power

Surrounded by
The tides of a deep heritage
Of Congress the pursuit of power

With a constitution
And a declaration of independence
Supporting this power

The statues stand
In buildings of stature
And Magnitude

In testimony to
How deep the American
Blood flows to gratitude

Flowing from strong
Dedicated men believing
In sovereign principles

With all others asked to be
As strong
But can they be sensible

Can they believe
As deeply
As America's blood flows

Are they more than
Themselves
Or just a picture of their ego

The phantoms of the Senate
Behind dappled desks
That stature bestows

Lining the marbled halls
The seats of power
Revered by shallow men

Distained by the weakling
Loved by idealists
Born from a belief in good fortune

A vein of gold
Inlaid upon a fallow land
Signifying the American heritage

A vein of obscurity
A vein of red white and blue blood
Flowing from the hearts of millions

Holding their leaders up to the light
To see if their ideals
Their principles with humility prevail

Tossing away those that are
Transparent and too flexible
To be the levy and the strength

To be our next heritage
The ides of a deep bondage
From the words at Gettysburg

To the dark shadow of Hiroshima
And the conquest of inner space
Far deeper than outer space

Senator oh Senator hearken
Hear this message or
Perish from the seat of power

You are not sacred
You are not above principle
You are only a human flower

Rooted in responsibility
To pledge allegiance
To our heritage that we empower

To you our Republic
For which it stands
One nation indivisible under God

With liberty and justice for all
So do not let the
Great American Enterprise fall

Don't do as the Romans did ... do you recall
Your oath that we must be free
To pursue opportunity for all
It is in that we entrust thee

The President, the Congress, the Rule of Law, the Constituency
For the sake of our forefathers, to protect our Good Earth's sod ...
So, help us God

PROGRESSIVES

*"A group, person, or idea favoring
or implementing social reform or new, liberal ideas"
... regardless of the cost*

*How can we be better
If we're all the same*

*Is a democracy capitalism
Or socialism or both*

*Is it the chicken or the egg
Is it the Republicans or the Democrats*

*Is it the uneven division of wealth
Or the division of Misery equally*

*Is it the cutting of the pork based on effort
Or the eating of the feast done by the least*

*Issues or problems how can anything be better
If we're all doled out our equal share*

*Take Education ... it covers a lot of ground but
Equality won't harvest any of it*

Like political rationalizations ... taxes are not the solution

*Take Health care ... it's better to cover it and
Not need it than to need it and not have it*

*Take Defense of country ... it's better to waste money
And not need the weapon than to have US wasted*

*Take Self-reliance – to those who do only what they please
Are seldom pleased with what they do*

*In the final analysis "if the good lord doesn't rule
The affairs of the people then tyrant's money will"*

How can we be better off
If we're all the same and getting soft

Give our brains and golf a challenge
And all of us will be better off

Give our bodies a lift and goal
We will prevent and preserve ourselves

How can we be better equal if we're all the same
We can't be better off if we are better equally

As we will all be lackadaisical meekly
And then Uncle Sam stops paying its bills weekly

OUR BINARY TWO-PARTY ESTABLISHMENT POLITICAL SYSTEM HAS FAILED US
(The two parties have built the swamp but are inept in draining or eliminating it)

The Roman Empire burned its future by ignoring its collective values and patriotism. While the Senate and Emperor argued the military wasted away it's honor on meaningless wars and land grabs. America is in the same spiral. As a result our cities are burning with Black Lives Matter and ANTIFA protests spiraling into uncivil riots, theft and destruction.

Reason: Both establishment parties are vying for control of Congress in 2022 mid-term elections by continuing polarized policies, regulations and gridlock. The Red and the Blue have become one party of purple. With the extremes becoming black and white revolutionaries.

Since the advent of the Great Society Programs we have evolved into a culture of violence, vulgarity and disproportionate excesses of prosperity divided by politics and media. I believe this is due to the failure of the leadership of our two establishment parties practicing money-tics not American enterprise values. Ask yourself, as a voter who would you pick a "better Red than dead pragmatic Republican" or a "Blue blood bleeding-heart phlegmatic Democrat" … or an "enterprising market driven American Enterprise Party Humanitarian" that wants every American citizen to be successful and healthy in pursing the American Utopian Dream.

With "go along to get along" establishment politics dominating our media, freedoms, relationships and congregating for holidays, shouldn't we have a say in the decisions making process? Of course, this is the foundation of representative government by the people, for the people, of the people but in reality, we have money-tics and the golden rule. "Those with the gold rule"! Our two-party establishment system is failing us in this regard. So, do we just acquiesce or desist? My America's vision says we need a representative party that persists on behalf of the 169 million enterprising Americans that effectively pay all the bills and 46 different taxes. My idea is a party that believes in and is patriotic to the 5 principles of governance that can prevail as the swing vote in our governing bodies, Presidency and Supreme Court. Those 5 principles of the American Enterprise Party are:

1. Balance the budgeting process using GAAP (generally accepted accounting principles) by downsizing government and up sizing enterprise.
2. Privatize health, environment and welfare funding using pay for performance outcomes justifying provider incomes and use conservation over depravation for changing the environment.
3. One vote with three alternatives pull the extremes to the one voice consensus in resolving national and local problems. Leaving issues to money driven politics.
4. Our reinforcement of the Rule of Law must be carried out by Governors who will provide incentives to policing and prosecutors to attain the peaceful coexistence and resolution of national and local problems.
5. The collective majority, with a patriotic voice, quiets the radical left and right minorities who are financed by anti-patriotism philosophy and counter culture policies.

FISCAL AND FINANCIAL FAILURE

The country is swamped in debt and past deficits ... bankrupt in all financial measures. American Federal and State debt exceeds our gross national product. The bubble has burst with $28 trillion in recorded debt and $158 trillion (www.usdebtclock.org) in unrecorded obligations ($470,200 dollars per citizen) and growing. Panic from the Covid-19 Pandemic has sunk our economic ship. We owe our future to competing enemies ($7 trillion dollars owed to foreign interests), $2.4 billion dollars spent on entitlements per year and debt exceeding our national GDP. Using GAAP (Generally Accepted Accounting

Principles), how are we to survive when we have 22 million government workers drawing record salaries (50% higher than the private sector).

A one trillion dollar per year payroll with $880 trillion dollars in unfunded pension costs for having full pensions even when retiring early, best of the best fully paid for health care and a separate social security funding for longevity. Plus, the Federal Reserve, a separate entity to protect their member banks, is gambling taxpayers' 401.k money on Treasury Bills and $570 trillion dollars in derivatives to fund the national debt. Then manipulates the interest rates ($3.9 trillion dollars in interest paid on national debt) without regard to inflating or deflating the American economy while America self-destructs with prices escalating and the value of the dollar plummeting. And a well-established elitist two-party establishment political system of governance that fiddles while America burns. Read the American Enterprise Manifesto in Volume II, by Jerry Rhoads to get the full bailout and reorganization plan.

HEALTH, ENVIRONMENT AND WELFARE FAILURE

The country as a whole isn't physically and mentally healthy. Exemplified by the Covid-19 Pandemic fear prevails at every level. Why, because the majority of Americans, according to the CDC and WHO aren't practicing healthy lifestyle habits. Their immune system is being attacked by any mutating virus. Sixty percent don't regularly exercise, forty percent are obese, twenty-five percent are depressed because of the Pandemic. Our health care system is upside down when it gets paid for illness not wellness. Lives lost to the Covid-19 Virus is secondary to the chronic illnesses that afflict 117 million Americans including 77 million baby boomers. All generations are dependent on prescription drugs and chemicals that are damaging our immunity and lowering our collective life expectancy.

Our environment of climate, storms, forest fires and waste are contaminating our earth and cities. This is collectively costing Americans $4.2 trillion dollars annually ($14,500 dollars per person) plus anticipated cost of emission controls. According to worldwide metrics, America is number one in health care per capita costs and thirty-eighth in quality of health… as life expectancy is going down for the first time ever. On the other hand, Singapore, a nation of five million people is number one in quality and last in cost per capita. Why are they better? Because they have a collaboration between individual funded universal insurance, government administration of the rules and collective funding of the safety nets for their aging and indigent population.

CONSENSUS AND CONSTITUTIONAL FAILURE

The constitution is being attacked by the left and the right factions of the political parties. Democrats support bigger government. Republicans stands for bigger business corporations; both with political contributions from Big Box, Big Media, Big Pharm, Big Tech, Big Energy. A diabolical binary gridlock that leaves working Americans in the middle of an endless fight that perpetrates doubt and hate. Our elections aren't open to the silent majority (169 million enterprising Americans) because it takes wealth to even run for local office and more to stay in any office with 90% of incumbents are reelected.

The country is run by the gang of 545 (100 senators, 435 congressmen, 9 supreme court justices and 1 president) using 50/50 Gridlock by no term limits , filibuster and contentious debate run by lobbyists. Voters are rallied using a social media and news media as their only source of fake and partisan rhetoric leaving our system of checks and balances in limbo. Correspondingly, the tech giants are using a Social Media delusion with algorithm marketing strategies selling users sublimated mind trackers as advertising. Turning the human mind into a robotic emotional buyer and voter.

JUSTICE AND EQUITY FOR ALL FAILURE

Our justice system has taken to the streets. It's now a fight of the ism's. Racism, socialism, fascism, media-ism forgetting humanism. Protests disguised as revolutionaries further divide the silent majority into two waring political establishment parties. The banners of discontent are leading America down the civil revolution track funded by those tech companies that are controlling America's media news culture. The underpinning of the revolt is money according to the golden rule ... those with the gold rule. Billionaires, info techs and corporate conglomerates use their gold and social media and news media for mind control to rule our so-called democratic elections.

None of this results in equality or equity. It merely takes from the majority of the voters its intentions and fair treatment while blaming each other for the problem. Resulting in the George Floyd hate crime being immortalized into a defund the police, woke allegations that all whites are racists, American history needs to be rewritten as critical race theory and our cultural icons be erased and replaced by the 1619 project as the start of our great country ... one year before the pilgrims arrived in 1620 at Plymouth Rock in Pennsylvania countering 1776 as our countries birth. Bringing equity to the slaves and eliminating any semblance of rational American history.

PATRIOTIC AND PEACEFUL COEXISTENCE FAILURE

As our society self-indulges in our social media and believes the fake news media our cultural values deteriorate. Also, our health habits ingest pills with dramatic side effects, legalized recreation drugs addict us, violence and vulgarity in our viewing and listening media erodes our values, excessive incomes of a few and poverty incomes for the many allows money to rule. With this failure we lose our honor and faith in what's Right by not knowing what's Left. We are polarized. By distortions of the truth, we effectively, no longer have a center in our lives or political system. Peaceful coexistence is lost to wealth. We have been misled by leaders of the political parties, who can afford or raise a billion-dollar run for the Senate, the House, the Presidency and win the Super Bowl, that anyone can compete for a seat of power. Leaving 169 million enterprising Americans that effectively pay all the bills and Federal and State taxes behind, to fight over the spoils of the establishment two-party failure.

WHAT'S THE SOLUTION TO STOPPING THE SPIRAL OF THE AMERICAN DREAM? THE AMERICAN ENTERPRISE PARTY BRINGS CAPITALISM AND SOCIALISM AS HUMANISM TOGETHER INTO THE GREAT AMERICAN ENTERPRISE. www.americanenterprisepoliticalparty.org

To avoid burning down our future and cities with protests, uncivil riots and violence we need a new governing philosophy.

1. **Fiscal and financial responsibility** ... by not using GAAP for our financial, taxation and budgetary system we have cooked the books

so the American people are led to believe that America is above accountability. But we are a country of laws and law enforcement. To that end our political parties argue over funding our military and police. Forgetting that our budget, on the accrual basis, needs to finance our collective health, welfare and education. None of these are free or replaceable by a Waring Congress or Nation. Consequently, each of us must earn our right to these inalienable rights by taking responsibility for our share of the decision making and cost. Without our approval, the gang of 545 wastes our national resources on $9 trillion dollars on regime wars, $3 trillion dollars on weapons of mass destruction (we hope we never use), $800 billion dollars of interest accrued on the national debt and $6 trillion dollars stimulus and masks/PPE funding of our unhealthy American lives.

A third party that stands for humanism and peaceful coexistence in a world of violence will prevail in leading those axes of evil towards peaceful coexistence. We then can focus on paying down the unsustainable spiraling $84 trillion national debt, $158 trillion of unrecorded obligations for pensions and entitlements legislated for all levels of our government. The wealthiest individuals, corporations and foundations who have profited from the Great American Enterprise must step up and reinvest equity in the Enterprise by lowering our dependence on debt that is leading to our collective self-destruction. A third party that stands for these principles can impact America's future by being the swing vote, 5 to10 seats in the Senate, 15 to 20 seats in the House and a seat in the Supreme Court and ultimately the Presidency. To that end America for all prevails.

2. **Health, environmental and welfare responsibility** … we are a country of failing collective health and welfare. An unhealthy and environmentally endangered America is an unacceptable condition when the world is looking to us to be the leader in those cultural attainments of the American Dream that lure the immigrant masses to our borders. A healthy American with a healthy environment, is an enterprising American that can proudly exercise the right to vote for a party that makes that principal a priority. America needs to be number one in quality of life and number one in return on our investment in universal health care services. Unfortunately, it is now costing Americans $4.2 trillion dollars annually ($14,500 per

person) for substandard health care services falling victim to billions of dollars wasted. To do this requires each and every American to be responsible for their own health, environmental and welfare costs through health savings accounts funded by employee withholding and an employer match representing the benefit.

3. By internalizing what it costs makes each of us discriminating consumers who hold the providers of the services accountable for cost, prices and outcome. Then the profit incentive can drive our health, environmental and welfare services to improving our collective standing in the world. Effectively, shifting the paradigm from government-controlled health care and environmental services to private funding and administration. Using collaboration, as the economic and societal solution.

Example: The worldwide environmental controls, espoused by the socialists, embrace fear and deprivation as the way to change the earth by garnering control over all national resources and dictating human behavior. Do we really think we mortals can save the Earth from its evolution by revolution? According to progressives the solution to the so-called climate change "issue" is to make it a problem then embrace an agenda where the many are controlled by a few for policies and behavioral laws.

Example the Pandemic where individual freedoms were replaced by edicts from government bureaucrat scientists using nonscientific methods for predicting disastrous deaths and deprivation that didn't bend the curve or save everyone. It merely put off the inevitable where a capitalist would save socialist lives with "warp speed" using his entrepreneurial skills to save all lives. Ironically deposed President Trump is the hero not Dr Fauci or Governor Cuomo or defecto President Joe Biden or Senator Bernie Sanders or Congresswoman AOC or Senator Elizabeth Warren. Aha, a lesson lived is a lesson learned, that a third party based on enterprise will also save the Republic, our land and the good earth.

OUR LAND

Kiss the Land... watch Netflix Video

The land upon which we walk
The land upon which our boot heels tread
The land upon which our hands guide the stalk
The land upon which we lay our dead

This land is ours while we're here
This land will give as much as it can take
This is why we must hold it oh so dear
Leaving it in place for our children's sake

The land is so beautiful in the spring
Holding to its breast the voice of nature
Uplifting with life to bring
For without it there would be no creature

We cultivate its fertility
We seem to ignore its scarcity
We find hope in its stability
And when it's over we inherit its sanctity

In the summer we watch the crops
Bloom into the harvests
Hoping that the cycle never stops
Providing food to feed our nests

Its green and black skin is only the surface
God is there no doubt
Beneath is our spirit and our purpose
Spreading life all about

In the fall as the leaves settle to the land
Getting ready to go to sleep
Why don't mortals understand
Why nature's children need peace to keep

Times have told us to feed the land
Don't forsake it just for today

Replenish thus our contraband
Lest the very soul of man will decay

As the winter curtain drops its veil
Over the eyes of those that hibernate
The cycle slows to almost stale
Putting us humans in a blissful state

Our land must stand and never fall
The land is the very roots of everything
The land is the soul of mother and father of all
The land has so much more to which we cling

So dig the black dirt and drop the seed
Pick its fruit
And curse its weed
But please don't forego the shoot

To sing out to nature's creed

"Your land is my land
Yours to till at my will
If you use it
God be damned if you
Abuse it"

With this statement of convenient truth
Supported by all even the youth
That our Good Earth our roots
Must sustain its natural worth

Through our committed conservation
Reading the signs of deterioration
Knowing salvation isn't deprivation
But needs an alliance of each nation

To serve Mother Nature's rule
As all individual's conserve
Then preserve her jewel
For our very survival's nerve

To each his own way
Our land holds all on Judgement Day

CONSERVE THE EARTH

The convenient truth is common sense
The earth manages its own events

Huffing and puffing our way through life
Fighting ourselves and our wife
Wending our way through strife
Sharpening our skills like a knife

Finding that wind has no beginning
Or end
So why do we deny our sinning
And the lack of support to defend

Curtailing of the waste
And garbage of our culture
Turning our environment in haste
To a plate for the vulture

Would it be different
If life were dependent upon
The contributions spent
For the spires built under the sun

Yes produce for the harvest
Each of us is to entrust
In the system and digest
Contributions to preservation or bust

Yes living in peace
Worldwide for mankind
While wars can cease
If the wind mills save our behind

Nor does climate change mean the end
And the earth can't be made to mend
Even if Mother Nature is our friend
And Father time shall descend

Self-destruction won't be ours to defend

Otherwise we are victims
Of ourselves
Tearing out the stems
Of Mother Nature as humanity sells

Out the environment
To a windless burnt earth
Only to awake to a wind event
Blowing across Hell's hearth

Waiting for the Savior's rebirth
The convenient truth is common sense
The earth manages its own events
We mortals must manage our own repents

4. **Consensus and Constitutional Responsibility** ... we have a system where constitutionally each of us have a say through our political parties. Presently, we have evolved into a system of "to get along go along" without consensus. Gridlock, filibuster and impeachment are the tools of fools who want us to believe that money talks. Consequently, the Red and Blue aren't providing a functional culture of rational debate for solving our collective national failures. The silent majority of Americans aren't being served as the voice of America when it takes wealth to run for any office. Our Big social media and Big news media using their technological methods are controlling the minds of the voters. The dilemma is their verbal and sublimated computer algorithms that are turning our minds into robotic responses to certain simulators that control our decision making. Thus, we have a purple Congress, Supreme court and Presidency. To serve the Red, White and Blue flag we need a third party representing 169 million enterprising Americans and their families. Or control of our future is in the hands of a dystopian political system promising each of us utopia,

using our compromised minds, to turn us against rational decision making for the greater good.

5. **Justice and Equity for All Responsibility** …. In our democracy we collectively are to honor nondiscrimination in carrying out enforcement of our laws. When we question the effectiveness of our system of justice with protests and anarchy, we must rethink our history and justice system. The indiscriminate use of force typically results in harm to the victim or the perpetrator, while reinforcement compromises anger with humanistic resolution. Our military and police will better serve us with peaceful coexistence in such confrontations … with no loser or winner so each party can feel justified in resolving their emotional acting out. This requires leadership that stands for principles of peaceful coexistence. This isn't sustainable, where race, and our caste system of poverty, are infuriating the dysfunctional neighborhoods that are run by gangs and crime. Until our inner cities have opportunity and prosperity, we won't have peaceful coexistence. By fulfilling the promise that all Americans have equal opportunity to attain the American Dream takes a third party standing for and competing for votes. It takes seats in Congress and State legislatures to attain equality for housing, education, conservation and jobs. And respect for all races, genders, faiths and beliefs turns enforcement into a reinforcement system of incentives for humanism and peaceful coexistence.

GIVE ME MY RIGHTS

Born to be free of tyranny equally

I was born on Thanksgiving Day
Baptized on Christmas Day
Raised in a free country somewhat stable
And given the opportunities available

To each sunrise I rose
And as soon as I could stand up and walk
I began chasing whatever I chose
Taking responsibility for what I stalk

And if I play seek and find
I couldn't really blame another
Not even my dad or mother
It was I who chose where I signed

For it was up to me
I really didn't contemplate or tout
That making the most of being free
Is putting my hand out

Or expecting equality from the State
I could stand on my own two feet
Taking care of myself was my family's fate
And the bills I had to meet

Yes freedom to me was an opportunity
But I guess I'm "out of sorts"
Not understanding the system of torts
Nor the courts as a handout of immunity

For they seem to be stating some deed
And protection under the law
About freedoms guaranteed
That "kind of hang up" in my craw

For Democracy is not a guarantee
Of freedom and equality
It's merely an opportunity for you and me
And those who choose and demand to be free

Most likely some lives are the pits
Though they may lose from their toils
Or are the pathetic hypocrites
Upon which pity spoils

Even though they can climb up on their back legs
With hands out and a lowly soul that begs
I must ignore them for what they are
With their hand in someone else's cookie jar

Barking and begging on their back legs
They're saying I demand equality
I've got the right for my country's free
And our "tis of thee" opportunity

Though we're supposed to have democracy
Guaranteeing everything to me
So give me my rights to this I demand
And to that to which I stand

Here in this dissolving quick sand
Of patricians under a flag of the red blue and whites
Impairing America's ability to demand
That all living here have to earn their rights

To this Plato understood
Unto which democracy stood
"Where even dogs would want to be free
Standing on their hind legs demanding equality"

And they're never going to be free
Because it takes an acquiring mind to pursue opportunity
In our land of "tis of thee"
Not just for you or me

But for all three
Peace, prosperity and equity

6. **Patriotic and Peaceful Coexistence Responsibility** ... We have won and protected our country's sovereignty with patriotism since 1776. This is built on our Fiscal stability, Individual Health, Consensus of principles, and Justice for All responsibility fulfilled. If any of these five principles fail then our establishment two-party system is at fault. Money then becomes the problem and a threat to our constitutional government. In any debate where rational resolution is lost to money and power a third-party opinion must be the swing vote. I repeat, it splits the independents away from the Democrats and the Republicans so neither has a majority. So, a third party does not assure any of the three parties a 51% majority allowing for the filibuster to really mean better legislation

and laws. Then we honor our Democratic System of checks and balances by hearing out the majority of 169 million enterprising Americans who effectively pay all the bills and the majority of 46 different Federal and State taxes who need a collective voice to act as a patriotic system of consensus that prevails over wealth and disproportionate financial influence.

THE NEW GOVERNMENT PHILOSOPHY REQUIRES A THIRD PARTY (with the following six principles)

An effective third political party that stands for national, fiscal, physical and mental health responsibility, consensus of the governed, justice for all, patriotism in war and the pursuit of peaceful coexistence must have a seat in governance. Consisting of Congress, State Legislatures, Supreme Courts and in the election of a President, Senator, Congressman, Governor, Councilmen, etc.

1. Balance the budgeting process using GAAP (generally accepted accounting principles) by downsizing government and up sizing enterprise.
2. Privatize health, education, environment and welfare funding using pay for performance outcomes justifying provider incomes. Conservation over depravation for changing the environment.
3. One vote with three alternatives pull the extremes to the one voice consensus in resolving national and local problems.
4. Our reinforcement of the Rule of Law must be carried out by Governors who will provide incentives to policing and prosecutors to attain the peaceful coexistence and resolution of national and local injustice problems.
5. The collective majority with a patriotic voice quiets the radical left and right minorities who are financed by anti-patriotism philosophy and policies.
6. We must have our Federal and State government report card, based on finances, taxation and budgeting on GAAP accrual basis of accounting, to be used as our management accountability report for the President, Congress, Courts, State Governors and constituents to judge our progress and the basis for problem solving.

IN SUMMARY

Currently, our country is a simulation of the rise and fall of Rome. Patriotically, we savor our right to battle radical socialism, capitalism, racism, elite ism when they attack our American Dream. While America is burning financially, wasting our health, environment and welfare, electing officials that honor the American money machine, without true justice or patriotism democracy is the real victim to the establishment two-party rule. To quote George Orwell in Animal Farm "the comrade Pigs spoke and over threw the dictator Farmer saying equality is for all comrades but some are more equal than others And subsequently in 1984 "Big Brother rule by the Few in the Brotherhood shall rule the Many for the sake of the fatherland" ... and of course a progressive or Marxist government Is pulling us closer to the Brave New World as depicted by Aldous Huxley.

1984

George Orwell predicted in 1984 the world
Would be run by Big Brother and Brotherhood ...where
War is peace
Ignorance is strength
Slavery is Freedom

1985 is far away
It could be tomorrow
Or even the next day

1984 has been quite a year
Filled with Big Brother
And a touch of Orwell's fear

Big Brotherhood took over as you know
They put down the dissidents
And the overthrow

Revolution instead of evolution
That's what we've got now
Only doing what they'll allow

They took the lion
Out of the roar
During that coup of 1984
Well even so
It's good to be alive
Hoping for freedom
In eighty-five

Back to the good ole days
Back to the freedom of thought
And healthier ways
Loyalty is earned not bought

Big Brother is Biden
The Brotherhood of Bigger is Better
America is too Big to Matter
unless
Peace is America
Freedom is Enterprise
Strength is Democracy

Vote American Enterprise Party

But no matter where
You go and what you do
There's no way to make
History new

So we have lived
Through reality in 1984
Until we close the door
And have hope for more

Looking to eighty-five
To bring hope and love back alive
So freedom of thought
Can once more thrive

Even though Orwell's prediction
Failed to arrive

Ironically, neither has happened yet in America but it is capitalism that funds and sustains our businesses while socialism is employing our human capital in enterprises for our collective economic fulfillment of the American Dream. Neither should be subservient to the other. So, why is our current Red and Blue Senate, House, Courts, and Presidency hell bent on treating them as enemies to our future and are complacent as America spirals into Orwellian dystopia and political nepotism. I believe it is our own success that is blinding us to the reality that it is a worldwide war of economies not armies. And we've been the rabbit and China the hare just waiting for us to self-destruct under the burden of our own ineffective establishment two-party system. In the wings are Japan, India, South Korea, Mexico, Russia and the Arab Spring waiting for the spoils to be parsed out.

I repeat for the third time … Ask yourself, as a voter who would you pick a "better Red than dead pragmatic Republican" or a "Blue blood bleeding-heart phlegmatic Democrat" … or an "enterprising market driven American Enterprise Party Humanitarian" that wants every American citizen to be successful and healthy in pursing the American Utopian Dream.

Why America Needs an Effective Third Political Party aS a Swing Vote

(To Drain the Swamp and Reign in Big Brother and the Brotherhood)

To quote George Orwell in Animal Farm "the comrade Pigs spoke and over threw the dictator Farmer saying equality is for all comrades but some are more equal than others". And subsequently in 1984 "Big Brother and the Brotherhood shall rule so the Few will overrule the Many for the sake of the fatherland."

THE GREAT AMERICAN ENTERPRISE NEEDS A SWING VOTE by Jerry Rhoads proposes a third political party; an American Enterprise Party that represents enterprising Americans and privatized agencies that downsizes government and up-sizes free market enterprise. With capitalism (money) and socialism (workers) working together as humanism to perpetuate the Great American Enterprise founded on policies that reduces laws, regulations, redundancy, debt, waste and deficits by following generally accepted accounting principles. Then, the three parties are able to better manage, under constitutional government, the finances and resources so our Great American Enterprise can be preserved.

The Red (capitalists) and Blue (socialists) extremes will be, by swing voting, pulled towards the middle by the White stars and stripes representing enterprising American voters. It splits the independents away from the Democrats and the Republicans so neither has a majority. So, a third party does not assure any of the three parties a 51% majority allowing for the filibuster to really mean better legislation and laws.

Then, by having the red, white and blue flag represented and using generally accepted accounting principles to finance environment change, we can balance the books, pay down secured debt and budget for surpluses using a budgetary system of cash in and cash out. At the same time, pursue world peace and solve the problems surrounding violence and poverty in America and the world.

A TYRANNICAL ATTACK ON CONSTITUTIONAL GOVERNMENT
(If you think H.R.1 and S 1 voting rights bills 2021 are Marxist, this is worse)

NEW YORK TIMES
By David Leonhardt June 16, 2021

Good morning. Ranked-choice voting is growing. We offer a strategic explainer.

A different kind of election

New York City's mayoral campaign is one of the highest profile instances of a ranked-choice election in the U.S. Rather than selecting only one candidate, voters can instead choose up to five and rank them.

The system has some big advantages. In a traditional election, people who vote for a long-shot candidate — like Ralph Nader, the Green Party presidential nominee, in 2000 — can end up hurting a top-tier candidate — like Al Gore that year. With ranked choice, progressive voters could have listed Nader first and Gore second. Once Nader failed to finish in the top two, the final round of the election would have reallocated his voters to their second choice, which often would have been Gore.

(Ranked choice is also known as instant-runoff voting, because people vote only once. The various "rounds" of voting all occur during the counting of ballots.)

The basic idea is to allow people both to select their favorite candidate and to indicate their preferences among the other candidates.

That combination can allow the most broadly popular candidate to win the election, while also making clear the full spectrum of voters' views. If Nader had received, say, 20 percent of first-place votes in 2000, it could have signaled the appeal of his platform and inspired other progressives to run in 2004.

For these reasons, ranked-choice voting can seem as if it eliminates the need for strategic voting. But it doesn't. Even with ranked choice, voters sometimes should consider more than their own preferences.

Today's newsletter offers an explainer — and not just because of New York. Ranked choice <u>has been growing recently</u>, with Maine using it in federal elections since 2018 and Alaska set to begin doing so next year. More than 50 cities — including Oakland, San Francisco and Minneapolis — have also decided to use it, as have state parties in Kansas, Virginia and elsewhere.

Ranked choice has obvious appeal when many people are <u>dissatisfied</u> with establishment politicians and parties.

Commentary by Jerry Rhoads, Author and Founder of AEP:

In my opinion, this is just another idea and mechanism by the progressive Democrats to bypass the constitutional electoral college and put their candidates in front with their name recognition and money-tics financed by Big Brother and the Brotherhood. The only way to stop this progressive/Marxist movement is to win the third-party swing vote position. Rank-choice voting is going to divide the nation beyond recognition allowing the powerful Few to continue to control the weaker Many, without accountability for America's future.

This will result in a one-party government. Therefore, vote for the American Enterprise Party, with its enterprising American patriots and their work ethic, to save the Great American Enterprise.

BIG BROTHER DEEP STATE SWAMP ACCOUNTING RESULTS

The cost of governance, including the health care of Americans, is currently lost to concealing reality by cooking the books. Not all of the obligations are recorded as incurred and revenues are recorded in advance of being earned; resulting in understating the cost of governance and overstating the amount of revenue collected for any period of time, due to accounting differences. The only reliable source of financial information, to answer the great economic questions, are embodied in the debt clock (www.usdebtclock.org) maintained by the US Chamber of Commerce in New York city. It, in real time, calculates the expenditures, tax receipts, debt and deficits, properly using generally accepted accounting principles (GAAP), a modified accrual method for government entities.

Instead of the annual deficit for 2020 being $6 trillion, it is $12 trillion, and the debt being 28 trillion, is $158 trillion after accruing unrecorded obligations that apply to the 2019 and 2020 taxation deficit. The covid-19 Pandemic will put America another $5.7 trillion in the hole. And putting the value of our currency and ability to pay our bills further in the red. Presuming, that the vaccines and therapies work going forward and our economy reverses itself, 2021 still will not get America above water due to the current accounting method used. This will be exacerbated, by the change in the establishment ruling party to Democrats controlling the House with a slim margin in the Senate by vote of the VP Harris, and our current governance will continue to be in gridlock. Unless the Republicans can recapture one or both houses in the midterms thus, opening up the opportunity for a reelected Trump and/or an effective third party in 2024. This requires the Republicans to rally behind a defrocked Donald J. Trump, as a Republican with 18 challengers for the throne , or realize he doesn't represent what the American Enterprise Party is offering.

Think about it . . . the $1.7 trillion college debt is more than the total credit card debt . . . since education is the route out of debt, catch 22 has just caught up with the graduates who cannot find a job or make their payments (2020 unemployment rate for ages 25 to 34 26.2%) . . . to placate them the progressive politicians, propose to write-off the debt and provide free college education while the regressive politicians demand equity to protect the right to file bankruptcy and earn an education.

The Establishment Two-Party Politics: America Is Now the Divided Republic the Framers Feared ... John Adams worried that "a division of the republic into two great parties ... is to be dreaded as the great political evil." And that's exactly what has come to pass.

The future is now or else ... asking for Enterprising Americans to stand up for equality and equity or we will fall for anything. Together we can prevail, divided we have fallen prey to the two-party establishment system of huge government control destroying the American Dream.

The American Dream: ideals of freedom, equality, and opportunity traditionally held to be available to every American with a life of personal happiness and material comfort traditionally sought by all individuals in the United States of America.

The American Nightmare: loss of freedom to oppressive two-party establishment Government regulations, debt and high taxes. For sake of argument, I reiterate the critical tipping point for America:

America's debt clock (www.usdebtclock.com) US 2020 federal spending $6.6 trillion, deficit $4.4 trillion, recorded debt $28 trillion ($84,000 per citizen), Medicare $1.3 trillion, Medicaid $1.1 trillion, Defense $720 billion, Interest on debt $392 billion, Federal pensions $300 billion, Agriculture subsidies $205 billion, total State, Federal and local spending $10.1 trillion (percent of GDP 47%), US GDP $21.2 trillion, total workers' compensation $11.5 trillion,

US Federal tax revenue $3.4 trillion, ($10,440 per citizens/$27,000 per taxpayer), tax revenue to GDP 15%, US spending to GDP 31%, tariff tax $70 billion, US trade deficit $867 billion, China $300 billion, US imported oil $100 billion,

The top 1% wealth $60.8 trillion, bottom50% wealth $1.8 trillion, small business assets $12.8 trillion, corporate assets $15.4 trillion, household assets $127 trillion, Social security liability $20.9 trillion, Medicare liability $32.4 trillion, US unfunded and unrecorded liabilities $158.7 trillion ($479,000 per citizen) as of now.

Yes, America is sitting on a $600 trillion-dollar derivative bubble called the American GDP, trade deficit with the stock market as the report card. When the cash flow is the Federal Reserve printing press and the progressive Democrats wanting to increase the bubble by $100 trillion over the next ten years (with higher taxes, free college education, free health care for all, forgiveness of college debt, emissions reduced to zero, $15 minimum wage, guaranteed minimum annual salary, total infrastructure over haul, two to three new states, open borders, amnesty for illegal immigrants (more voters, criminals and imbedded terrorists), lower the voting age to sixteen, do away with the electoral college, redistrict voting for minorities, extend the term limit of a sitting president to a decade, reduce military spending, extend retirement age to 75 for Social Security and Medicare benefits and expand foreign aid to progressive third world countries) we will find out that Build Back Bigger is never Better. It's bogus.

WHAT'S BETTER? A third party with an agenda to downsize government at all levels and upsize American Enterprise for all. Aka enterprise third party www.americanenterprisepoliticalparty.org

The Bigger the Government the Smaller American Enterprise. The Biden "Build Back (Bigger) Better" policies will be the financial straw that breaks the American Dream's back. According to his plan taxes to the wealthy will be increased to pay for a $2.2 trillion infrastructure bill. However, since this will only raise enough to pay interest on the new debt the Federal Reserve will have to print up new currency instruments, including a 100 year treasury bond. Then the takeaways begin. Entitlements, national security, health care for all, freedom of speech and protection under the first and second amendments. The current leadership of Biden, Harris, Pelosi, Schumer, Sanders, Warren, etc., all Harvard or liberal attorneys, career politicians with no business acumen. Who cannot run an Enterprise the size of America or be competitive with the rest of the emerging economies of the world? Namely, China, South Korea, India, Germany, Mid East, Southeast Asia, Mexico and Canada. All of which are way more austere then America the Bigger boy on the block.

Quoted from the Atlantic article: America Is Now the Divided Republic the Framers Feared ... John Adams worried that "a division of the republic into two great parties ... is to be dreaded as the great political evil." And that's exactly what has come to pass.

JANUARY 2, 2020

This story is part of the project "The Battle for the Constitution," in partnership with the National Constitution Center. Author **LEE DRUTMAN** *is a senior fellow in the political reform program at New America and the author of Breaking the Two-Party Doom Loop: The Case for Multiparty Democracy in America*

"American democracy is at an impasse. After years of zero-sum partisan trench warfare, our political institutions are deteriorating. Our norms are collapsing. Democrats and Republicans no longer merely argue; they cut off contact with each other. In short, the two-party system is breaking our democracy, and driving us all crazy".

"Deftly weaving together history, democratic theory, and cutting-edge political science research, Drutman tells the story of how American politics became so toxic, why the country is trapped in a doom loop of escalating two-party warfare, and why it is destroying the shared sense of fairness and legitimacy on which democracy depends. He argues that the only way out is to have more partisanship-more parties, to short-circuit the zero-sum nature of binary partisan conflict. American democracy was once stable because the two parties held within them multiple factions, which made it possible to assemble flexible majorities and kept the temperature of political combat from overheating. But as conservative Southern Democrats and liberal Northeastern Republicans disappeared, partisan conflict flattened and pulled apart. Once the parties fully separated, toxic partisanship took over. With the two parties divided over competing visions of national identity, Democrats and Republicans no longer see each other as opponents, but as enemies. And the more the conflict escalates, the shakier our democracy feels".

"America has now become that dreaded divided republic. The existential menace is as foretold, and it is breaking the system of government the Founders put in place with the Constitution.

Though America's two-party system goes back centuries, the threat today is new and different because the two parties are now truly distinct, a development that I date to the 2010 midterms. Until then, the two parties contained enough overlapping multitudes within them that the sort of bargaining and coalition-building natural to multiparty democracy could work inside the two-party system. No more. America now has just two parties, and that's it.

The theory that guided Washington and Adams was simple, and widespread at the time. If a consistent partisan majority ever united to take control of the government, it would use its power to oppress the minority. The fragile consent of the governed would break down, and violence and authoritarianism would follow. This was how previous republics had fallen into civil wars, and the Framers were intent on learning from history, not repeating its mistakes.

James Madison, the preeminent theorist of the bunch and rightly called the father of the Constitution, supported the idea of an "extended republic" (a strong national government, as opposed to 13 loosely confederated states) for precisely this reason. In a small republic, he reasoned, factions could more easily unite into consistent governing majorities. But in a large republic, with more factions and more distance, a permanent majority with a permanent minority was less likely.

The Framers thought they were using the most advanced political theory of the time to prevent parties from forming. By separating powers across competing institutions, they thought a majority party would never form. Combine the two insights—a large, diverse republic with a separation of powers—and the hyper-partisanship that felled earlier republics would be averted. Or so they believed.

However, political parties formed almost immediately because modern mass democracy requires them, and partisanship became a strong identity, jumping across institutions and eventually collapsing the republic's diversity into just two camps.

Yet separation of powers and federalism did work sort of as intended for a long while. Presidents, senators, and House members all had different electoral incentives, complicating partisan unity, and state and local parties were stronger than national parties, also complicating unity.

For much of American political history, thus, the critique of the two-party system was not that the parties were too far apart. It was that they were too similar, and that they stood for too little. The parties operated as loose, big-tent coalitions of state and local parties, which made it hard to agree on much at a national level.

From the mid-1960s through the mid-'90s, American politics had something more like a four-party system, with liberal Democrats and conservative Republicans alongside liberal Republicans and conservative Democrats. Conservative Mississippi Democrats and liberal New York Democrats might have disagreed more than they agreed in Congress, but they could still get elected on local brands. You could have once said the same thing about liberal Vermont Republicans and conservative Kansas Republicans. Depending on the issue, different coalitions were possible, which allowed for the kind of fluid bargaining the constitutional system requires.

But that was before American politics became fully nationalized, a phenomenon that happened over several decades, powered in large part by a slow-moving post-civil-rights realignment of the two parties. National politics transformed from a compromise-oriented squabble over government spending into a zero-sum moral conflict over national culture and identity. As the conflict sharpened, the parties changed what they stood for. And as the parties changed, the conflict sharpened further. Liberal Republicans and conservative Democrats went extinct. The four-party system collapsed into just two parties.

The Democrats, the party of diversity and cosmopolitan values, came to dominate in cities but disappeared from the exurbs. And the Republicans, the party of traditional values and white, Christian identity, fled the cities and flourished in the exurbs. Partisan social bubbles began to grow, and congressional districts became more distinctly one party or the other. As a result, primaries, not general elections, determine the victor in many districts.

Over the past three decades, both parties have had roughly equal electoral strength nationally, making control of Washington constantly up for grabs. Since 1992, the country has cycled through two swings of the pendulum, from united Democratic government to divided government to united Republican government and back again, with both sides seeking that elusive permanent majority, and attempting to sharpen the distinctions between the parties in order to win it. This also intensified partisanship.

These triple developments—the nationalization of politics, the geographical-cultural partisan split, and consistently close elections—have reinforced one another, pushing both parties into top-down leadership, enforcing party discipline, and destroying cross-partisan deal making. Voters now vote the party, not the candidate. Candidates depend on the party brand. Everything is team loyalty. The stakes are too high for it to be otherwise.

The consequence is that today, America has a *genuine* two-party system with no overlap, the development the Framers feared most. And it shows no signs of resolving. The two parties are fully sorted by geography and cultural values, and absent a major realignment, neither side has a chance of becoming the dominant party in the near future. But the elusive permanent majority promises so much power, neither side is willing to give up on it.

Read: How American politics went insane

This fundamentally breaks the system of separation of powers and checks and balances that the Framers created. Under unified government, congressional co-partisans have no incentive to check the president; their electoral success is tied to his success and popularity. Under divided government, congressional opposition partisans have no incentive to work with the president; their electoral success is tied to his failure and *un*popularity. This is not a system of bargaining and compromise, but one of capitulation and stonewalling.

Congressional stonewalling, in turn, leads presidents to do more by executive authority, further strengthening the power of the presidency. A stronger presidency creates higher-stakes presidential elections, which exacerbates hyper-partisanship, which drives even more gridlock.

Meanwhile, as hyper-partisanship has intensified legislative gridlock, more and more important decisions are left to the judiciary to resolve. This makes the stakes of Supreme Court appointments even higher (especially with lifetime tenure), leading to nastier confirmation battles, and thus higher-stakes elections.

The good news is that nothing in the Constitution requires a two-party system, and nothing requires the country to hold simple plurality elections. The elections clause of the Constitution leaves states to decide their own rules, and reserves to Congress the power to intervene, a power that Congress has used over the years to enforce the very plurality-winner single-member districts that keep the two-party system in place and ensure that most elections are uncompetitive.

Multiparty democracy is not perfect. But it is far superior in supporting the diversity, bargaining, and compromise that the Framers, and especially Madison, designed America's institutions around, and which they saw as essential to the fragile experiment of self-government.

America has gone through several waves of political reform throughout its history. Today's high levels of discontent and frustration suggest it may be on the verge of another. But the course of reform is always uncertain, and the key is understanding the problem that needs to be solved. In this case, the future of American democracy depends on heeding the warning of the past. The country must break the binary hyper-partisanship so at odds with its governing institutions, and so dangerous for self-governance. It must become a multiparty democracy." End of quote from the Atlantic article.

Money is the fuel that drives the Great American Enterprise System . . . Big Brother Government, and the Brotherhood of Big Media, Big Box, Big Tech, Big Money-tics, Big Unions, Big Pharma …

Money is the pendant of power that is the celebration of success or the crucifixion of our society's values as our mores and ethics become secondary to its use. What is our national self-worth, self-health, self-image, net-worth? Is it being misspent on power and control by a few? Can we sustain our national success when the few make promises they don't keep? Net worth or GNP or GDP are measures of our country's successes and failures when we evaluate our leaders. How do you rate them? Are you happy and confident that American Enterprise is in good hands. . . let's spend the next few hundred pages measuring our leaders' performance for a change.

Net worth, being a measure of performance, is defined as assets valued at the lower of cost or market value minus liabilities valued at the higher of cost or contingency. This formula is based on GAAP (generally accepted accounting principles) using the accrual basis of accounting. While taxes for individuals are generally paid on the cash basis which is collected income minus paid out allowable expenses (adjusted gross income) which is far different than net worth. Corporations, on the other hand, generally report taxable income using GAAP minus tax credits and accelerated depreciation methods.

THE BROTHERHOOD (Deep State)

The United Nations estimates that America's net worth including its human capital was $157 trillion in 2021 (which is 25.4% of worldwide net worth, 21.9% of worldwide GDP). Household net worth was estimated to be $54.2 trillion in 2009. 84% of that is controlled by 24% of the wealthiest Americans with Jeff Bezos net worth $200 billion, Mark Zuckerberg $103 billion, Bill Gates ($66 billion down from $89 billion) and Warren Buffet ($50 billion down from

$65 billion) the wealthiest individuals. The wealthiest corporations are Microsoft $1.7, trillion, Amazon $1.6 trillion, Apple $2.2 trillion, Exxon at $486 billion and Walmart at $600 billion with the Walton family heirs worth as much as the bottom 41.5 percent of Americans.

In the book that follows. it is proposed that any level of taxation based on adjusted gross income for individuals and net taxable income for corporations cannot and does not generate enough revenues to support government half its current size. This is because Governmental accounting is not based on GAAP but on the cash basis. What this does is allows government to understate its deficits and overstate its surpluses.

This illusionary method records the revenues that are accelerated using estimated taxes for the next year as current revenue and defers the recording of the cost of budgeted expenses until they are paid . . . in other words it overstates revenue that has yet to be earned and understates expenses by only recording them when paid not when they're owed . . . for example unfunded pension costs that have been earned by government employees are not recorded until paid . . . as is the case for entitlements.

THE DEEP STATE SWAMP REVISITED

Filing for Chapter 10 bankruptcy of the USA

Therefore, the current Federal deficit, as is the cooking of the books for every governmental unit, is far short of the real deficit . . . $158 trillion actual versus $28 trillion that is reported. While the annual excess of accrued expenses over earned, revenues is a minus $4.5 trillion for 2020 though reported as $13.2 trillion. The trade deficit is $916 billion (China $311 billion) per year. $6 trillion unfunded pension liability. Total State, local and Federal debt $82.6 trillion. Total debt held by foreign countries $7.1 trillion. Total interest on debt per annum $3.8 trillion. Total personal debt $21 trillion, mortgage debt $17.1 trillion, student loan debt $1.7 trillion, credit card debt $1.1 trillion putting total national debt on the accrual basis as $158.4 trillion with $157.3 trillion in national assets or a negative net worth of $1.1 trillion. Total Federal tax revenue of $3.5 trillion, State tax revenue $2.1 trillion, local tax revenue $1.5 trillion or a total national tax revenue of $7.1 trillion versus current expenses of $10.1 trillion or an annual deficit of $3 trillion plus 2020 Pandemic stimulus of $5.8 trillion on GDP of $21.6 trillion. For the first since world war two current Federal debt exceeds GDP by 129.7%.

The swamp exists at every State level with the Capitol as the top of the ant hill of money-tics. Currently the collective debt and accumulated deficits of the states is $10 trillion using GAAP and growing. For example: Each State has its own organization chart of locally staffed voters beholding to the current party in power. The State of Iowa, a Red State, has a patronage system of over 2,000 committees and sub committees ... all appointed by the party in power. Most of the committees have a budget and are paid for perfunctory activities at the local level that is nothing more than a system of political funding raising. The State of Illinois, a Blue State, has the same system of patronage but bigger. An effective third party would turn these patronage committees and subcommittees into fund raisers for community development and restoration of inner cities and under privilege small town's infrastructure projects so it is decentralized action groups contracting the employment of small to medium enterprises to keep America fit and healthy. Take it out of the hidden government for reelection of the same leaders and two parties and use it to save American Enterprise and restore the work ethic. As proven with the recent Biden 2021 stimulus payment of unemployment benefits that were more than salary levels, workers stayed home and there were 8 million open jobs waiting for them to return to the work force. This proves the adage that government does not create jobs it kills them when it gives out more than the recipient is making. Then Big Brother taketh away when all else fails.

This being the true situation demands what is called a quasi-reorganization to avoid bankruptcy. Under Chapter 11 (Chapter 10 for government entities) bankruptcy law individuals, corporations and other entities are allowed to reorganize their finances so they can avoid dissolution. The court appoints a trustee who directs the entity to propose a plan that will pay down its secured debt first then use whatever is left to pay off the unsecured creditors and investors. It also requires in the plan an infusion of new capital for allowing the entity the resources and time to go forward with its business in a responsible manner. This perpetuates the entity for producing future profits and putting it on a sound financial footing.

In the book it is proposed that Government at all levels is insolvent due to using cash basis accounting methods and accumulating deficits they can never liquidate, even with tax increases, without quasi-reorganization... meaning more equity capital and less current debt. (To prove my point, take a look at San Bernardino and Detroit). This capital can be generated by increasing taxes, cutting the size of its payroll and overhead down to the breakeven point and finding investors that will put capital into the entity to allow it time to reduce its costs and generate a true surplus. Increasing taxes is perpetuating the problem since it takes capital out of the American Enterprise for nonrevenue producing overhead costs.

Therefore, the only viable and accelerated method to put the Enterprise (government at all levels) back on its feet is to generate more capital to give America time to downsize government and upsize enterprise so the jobs are truly created and the profits and tax payers can increase earned revenues to pay accrued costs. Then the current net worth of the Enterprise (individuals and corporations, including not for profits) must be utilized in the reorganization. Using a 5% flat assessment on current net worth of individuals and corporations to generate the capital while eliminating taxes on adjusted gross income altogether for five years will put $25 trillion in the coffers. This can be used for paying down governmental debt while we privatize half of the Federal agencies that will become tax paying entities staffed by the private sector unemployed and the public sector employees as accountable businesses run by the shareholders. This puts taxable income for the future into the hands of the producers not the regulators.

MONEY-TICS AND POLITICS ARE BEDFELLOWS

Since our government is run on money-tics not politics, who are the targets for major infusion of capital (equity) into the Treasury to pay down unsecured foreign debt . . . the wealthy individuals and corporations that have generated their wealth from the work of enterprising Americans who now pay 46 different taxes. Following are examples of the public sector servants and corporations who have accumulated wealth at the cost of the Enterprise that, since the retraction of the gold standard backing our currency, has escalated deficits and debt approaching $158 trillion on a generally accepted accounting principles (GAAP) basis of accounting:

- Michael Blumberg net worth $50.1 billion.
- Donald Trump net worth of $3.1 billion.
- Joe Biden net worth of $9 million.
- Barak Obama net worth of $12.2 million, Michelle Obama $11.8 million.
- Bill Clinton net worth of $60 million, Hillary Clinton $21.5, Chelsea Clinton net worth of $15 million.
- George Soros net worth $8.3 billion philandrist and political operative.
- Georg Bush, jr. net worth of $35 million, George Bush, sr. $80 million.
- Ross Perot net worth $3.5 billion.
- John Kerry $194 million, Andrew Cuomo $9 million.
- Mitt Romney net worth $250 million, Mitch McConnell $9.2 million.
- Dianne Feinstein $70 million, Nancy Pelosi net worth $35.5 million, John Edwards $55 million, Chuck Schumer $1 million.
- Herb Kohl net worth $215 million, Jay Rockefeller $86 million.
- Newt Gingerich net%. worth $7 million.
- John and Cindy McCain $110.5 million.
- Chris Christie net worth $4 million, Paul Ryan $3 million.
- Sara Palin net worth $12 million, Al Gore $300 million.
- Harry Reid net worth $5 million, Jimmy Carter $5 million.
- Rahm Emanuel net worth $14 million.
- Grassley, Boehner, Biden, Justice Roberts, Charles Rangel, Barnie Frank all millionaires.
- Mark Cuban net worth $4.3 billion.
- Sports heroes signing Big Money contracts ... you know who they are ... Mahomes, King James, Mike Trout, Williams sisters, etc.
- Hollywood stars making more money than the movie box office ... Streep, Johnson, Affleck, Miranda, Jlo, Smith, Sandler, etc.

The top 1% wealth $60.8 trillion, bottom 50% wealth $1.8 trillion,

Currently, the Oligarch of 545 control the entire $118 trillion National net worth through lawmaking and political connections. The question is, does money-tics continue to use the golden rule ... those with the gold shall rule? Or will our constitutional government prevail with government of the people, by the people for the people. Welcome to the Brother Hood in the Land of the Few who use their money-tics to fund their enterprises and have not reinvested capital to allow the Great American Enterprise to pay down its delinquent debt. Now is the time to step up and save the Great American Enterprise.

Amazon World Services $1.6 trillion, Jeff Bezos net worth $200 billion
Microsoft net worth of $1.7 trillion, Bill Gates net worth of $66 billion,
Berkshire $500.6 billion, Warren Buffet $50 billion
Face book $732 billion, Mark Zuckerberg $103 billion
Twitter $40.8 billion, Jack Dorsey $11.2 billion
Zoom Video Technologies, $12 billion, Eric Yuan $35 billion
Google (Alphabet) $1.24 trillion, Larry Page $78.1 billion
Tesla Motors net worth, $770 billion, Elon Musk $185 billion
Exxon Oil net worth of $486 billion,
Walmart $447 billion, Walton family $86 billion
Apple Technology net worth of $2.2 trillion, Steve Jobs estate $10.6 billion
Home Depot $295 billion, Bernie Marcus $5.9 billion
Target $90.8 billion, Brian Cornell $116 million
CVS Pharmaceuticals $152 billion, Walgreens $43.7 billion
General Motors $50.7 billion, Fiat Chrysler $30.9 billion, VW $108.2 billion, Ford Motor Company $42.1 billion
Gross National Product $21.3 trillion (flat reinvestment in the Great American Enterprise at 5% per year of the net worth of Americans and American companies is $5 trillion per year for pay down of the national debt and generate balanced Federal, State and Local budgets in five years).

The Golden Rule is functioning as those with the Gold Rule ... the ruling class lords over the subjects or maybe it's objects. It's not socialism or communism yet. Until the two-party establishment binary Congress and Big Tech through the Big Social Media labeled an essential business during the Pandemic and never missed a paycheck, decides to limit freedom of speech and teams up to track down dissidents. This leaves the Many at the mercy of the Few until we enterprising Americans have the 21st century version of The Roman Empire. Until then...

God Bless America the land of the free, the land of the lawmakers who are destroying this freedom with 40,467 bills proposed across the country with an average of 25% written into law in 2012 that encumber the American Enterprise to another $200 billion per year to implement and police the Enterprise thereby increasing the deficit at the rate of $25 trillion per year. It is time to turn the tables and let the private sector grow and the public sector shrink under this plan of reorganization. As in any Enterprise, an unmanageable deficit triggers a need for capital infusion from its largest and wealthiest beneficiaries of America the Enterprise, be it loans or equity. And give a haircut to its largest creditors. China, Japan, South Korea, etc. In a world where we have the Golden Rule (those with the gold rule) redistribution of wealth is rejected by both the Red and the Blue but in effect graduated taxes, as a percentage of AGI income, is a redistribution.

Re-distribution of wealth is not proposed in this book. However, when the Great American Enterprise is under water and insolvent and cannot service its debt, equity capital is the only solution along with reduction of the reasons for the insolvency. So, it is the author's thinking, having been in his own business for 37 years, that those with the Gold have to step up and recapitalize the Enterprise as the quasi-reorganization takes place. We must Drain the Swamp, Reign in Big Brother and the Brotherhood to survive. At the same time the unsecured debt must be cut by 10% per year through downsizing expenditures for government employees and funding their pensions, foreign aid, support of the NATO, WHO, trade deficit, defense spending, foreign oil expenditures, clean energy initiatives, health care spending, increases in minimum wage, unemployment compensation, supplemented by collections of college debt and savings from privatized health care and education.

Like it or not our current lack of liquidity will destine us to losing out on technology because the public sector pensions, that are written into law, have to be funded and tax increases are the inevitable result of allowing a few with the gold to destroy, with the new entitlements, the American Work Ethic that creates the gold. So, this is not a redistribution of wealth but an investment in downsizing Government to private companies that will be accountable to the American Enterprise and pay dividends to those investing their Gold. This is true Enterprise taking back America from destructive Institutional Keynesian theory propagated by and controlled by the Gang of 545.

I have been told there is no way a third party can get elected for any political position. However, that's exactly what Margret Thatcher did that turned England around from overwhelming war debt, 90% taxation and an eroding standard of living to finance extreme socialism, that was killing off the Great Britain economy and position in the world. I was also told the likely hood this happening in America is proven by the failure of the Tea Party and Independent candidates over the years. However, the idea is to bring capital and the enterprising Americans together in a political party representing us all, that defuses what the two-party establishment hides from all of us… the very partnership that protects constitutional government enabling the American Dream to thrive again.

Then Democracy is to allow the freedoms of individuals, despite the color of their skin, religious beliefs and gender, to be political representatives regardless of wealth. The use of reinvestment of wealth into our economy to pay down the debt isn't redistribution of wealth but a refinancing of the great American Enterprise thereby functioning as the swing vote in Congress as the template for our State legislatures and other emerging countries around the world. It splits the independents away from the Democrats and the Republicans so neither has a majority. So, a third party does not assure any of the three parties a 51% majority allowing for the filibuster to really mean better legislation and laws.

IS FREEDOM A FALSE POSITIVE

Give me liberty or give me death ... Patrick Henry
Liberty being the right to be free to pursue opportunity

One cannot appreciate freedom
Till there is a prison door

No one can appreciate wealth
Till they become poor

No one can appreciate loyalty
Until they're royalty
No one can appreciate sadness
Until they are confronted with
Unadulterated badness

Overcoming imprisoned rift
Appreciated as a state of mind
A state you must seek as a gift
One false move and all is blind

For freedom to gain importance
There must be imprisonment
As the judges and bailiffs take their stance
Be it circumstance or happenstance

Binding our arms around our waist
Saying we're not free to speak think or impart
Living life in haste
Chasing those that tear out our heart

We're a slave they're the suitor
Throwing off the first amendment to teach
With a grave for failure of the tutor
To climb out of the casket called freedom of speech

Leaving most deaf and dumb
And to the sheep beseech
The true meaning of freedom
Left only to preach

For the negative sum of one
Be it defending our freedom
To speak up for Jim Crow (black Americans)
Enforcing the fifteenth amendment or foe
... with false hope in tow

To speak up for John Crow (white Americans)
Enforcing the First Amendment
We give in to a false positive
And hold court in the prisons
As truths fight to be alive
So that all can see the reasons

To make the right decisions
Social revolution for
Social injustice to restore
And unite Jim and John Crow
For being free is not unjust
Pursing opportunity is thus
Celebrating Juneteenth is u.s.

In the Great American Enterprise

This leaves the current liberal, conservative, left and right, Red and Blue extremism, progressive and regressive labels to focus on saving the Great American Enterprise and work toward peaceful coexistence for solving free market enterprise and crime in the street's problems. A patriotic affair to match the second World War victory in four short years and win the current China Cold War with the American Enterprise Party.

I repeat, our ammunition is American Enterprise that brings monetary capital and human capital together every day in American business to form a coalition not enemies. It takes capital to fund business and humans to manage those resources (assets, profits and cash flow) that are generated by this dynamic duo. Therefore, the need for the American Enterprise Party to fend off the extremes of the two-party establishment system and become **the swing vote** in arbitrating the divergence of the conservative and liberal, Red and Blue, left and right philosophies and policies that are destroying the Great American Enterprise. Make American Solvent Again. MASA … true liberty for all comes at a cost and profit.

The Untapped Power of the Swing Vote, by Linda Killian

About the Author

Linda Killian is a journalist and senior scholar at the Woodrow Wilson International Center for Scholars. She has been a columnist for Politico, U.S. News & World Report.com, and Politics Daily. She has also written for *The Washington Post, The New Republic,* and *The Weekly Standard,* among other national publications. Her previous book was *The Freshmen: What Happened to the Republican Revolution?* She lives in Washington, D.C.

The Swing Vote: The Untapped Power of Independents tells the story of how our polarized political system is not only misrepresenting America but failing it. Linda Killian looks beyond the polls and the headlines and talks with the frustrated citizens who are raising the alarm about the acute bi-polarity, special interest-influence, and binary gridlock in Congress, asking why Obama's post partisan presidency is anything but, and demanding realism, honest negotiation, and a sense of responsibility from their elected officials.

Killian paints a vivid portrait of the swing voters around the country and presents a new model that reveals who they are and what they want from their government and elected officials. She also offers a way forward, including solutions for fixing our broken political system. This is not only a timely shot across the bows of both parties but an impassioned call to independents to bring America back into balance.

Comments: This book has an array of earth-shattering comments from true patriots feeling the way I do and have acted upon it without breaking the good ole boys strangle hold on power. Declaring Independent as your third-party brand is like calling a Harley a bike. We need a brand that demands the involvement of patriots yes but also financial experts on governance by the Great American Enterprise who understand and believe the U.S. Chamber of Commerce debt clock www.usdebtclock.org and use it as the grade we give our failed (insolvent and bankrupt) two-party establishment system. But declaring our independence is not enough to bring all 200 million enterprising Americans to our party. Yes, it takes leadership and the guts to ...

Drain the Swamp
DiSpoSe of the AlligatorS
(Reign in Big Brother and the Brotherhood)

Former President Trump woke up the wokes when he proposed we drain the swamp and kill the alligators. In a gridlocked (no consensus) Congress, aren't the so called wokes, the alligators that wanted to dump Trump before he exposed the depth of the swamp's financial problems? So, the power of the two-party system, as predicted by our forefathers, benefits the Few at the cost of the Many. How deep is the swamp (Federal and State governments) and who are the Woke Alligators? The American Chamber of Commerce debt clock in New York City is the only source of transparency for watching second by second the expanse and depth of the swamp by each alligator www.usdebtclock.com The biggest alligators are:

- 22 million Federal, State and Local government employees' nationwide (LA's Homeless Dept of 20,000 employees making $120,000 per).
- $1.3 trillion annual payroll for government employees (salaries range from $125,000 to $63,000 per employee).
- $10.3 trillion employee benefits for government workers (includes accrued unfunded pension benefits for all current employees).
- $10.7 trillion annual deficit spending for Federal, State and local budgets.
- $82 trillion Federal, State and Local total debt.
- $158 trillion unfunded and under recorded liabilities.
- $20.7 trillion total personal debt.
- Total workers' compensation $11.5 trillion.
- 18 million unemployed, post pandemic 40 million.

- Federal unfunded pension liability $2 trillion, States unfunded pension liability $6.2trillion, local pension debt $2.1 trillion.
- Trade deficit $867 billion, China $300 billion.
- Student loan debt $1.7 trillion ($438,000 per student).
- Credit card debt $965 billion ($6,000 per holder).
- US GDP $21.2 trillion.
- Annual Federal tax revenue $3.4 total USA tax revenue $7 trillion,
- US spending to GDP 131%.
- 50 States run like fiefdoms, with redundancy between State Agencies and the Federal government, creating accumulated deficits, on a GAAP basis, of $1.3 trillion and growing at a rate of 20% per year. Resulting in total Federal, State and Local debt 145.4% of GDP and unfunded pension debt of $6.3 trillion.

In 2020 the Federal deficit reached a record $4.4 trillion, $4.2 trillion in health care costs and the recorded debt of $28 trillion, as of April fool's day 2021, due to the Pandemic and bailing out the economy for the shutdowns forced upon small businesses that weren't deemed as essential as were Big Brother government workers, Big Box stores, Big Media, Big Tech, Big Unions Big Pharma and the other largest corporations.

But this is just the tip of the proverbial iceberg … we need to work with all the facts we have at hand. With the new administration coming on and the country still polarized and divided on solutions to problems, not Congressional and political rhetoric on issues … this may permanently push us over the debt cliff with the decline in Federal and State tax revenues, higher cost of unemployment, cost of vaccines, masks and PPE draining the bank accounts, small businesses closing forever being replace by bigger and bigger box stores and tech companies warehousing data using sublimated algorithms and censoring tweets, YouTube and Facebook's arbitrary closing down of accounts and judging use of political disinformation. Add prices rising, profits plummeting and a progressive Administration proposing more taxes, free college education, defunding the police, write-off of college debt, changing the Supreme Court, increasing the minimum wage, free health care that threatens funding for health care entitlements. The ramifications are coming to roost:

(This all results from the new administration's policies implemented by executive orders and policy statements regarding canceling the

Keystone pipe line, opening the borders, allowing undocumented migrants to swarm into the country with no hinderance for the cartels to deal drugs and human trafficking, without Covid testing and a plan for integrating these unskilled workers into our struggling economy. By the end of 2021 this could mean 2 million such human problems are called issues between the two parties with no action taken to put the genie back in the bottle. It would seem the governors of the affected State borders should activate the national guard and stop the flow until it can be managed humanitarianly. Or let Nancy Pelosi send 25,000 troops to the borders to stop this national attack on our sovereignty, as she did at the Federal Capitol after January 6th. This being a hundred thousand percent bigger threat to our American sovereignty).

To help with financial and economic recovery the Chamber of Commerce maintains a Federal, 50 States, Local and international debt clock (algorithms update the data by the second) in New York City www.usdebtclock.org revealing comprehensive analytical data available for making visible American Federal and State financial and operational data for the purposes of managing the American Enterprise more effectively.

As I will quote figures throughout the books three volumes from this source, I advise anyone not concerned about America's future to be looking at the size of the Titanic-al sinking ship here and around the world. Me being a CPA, and financial-ologist (a CPA who believes any enterprise must use GAAP for true transparency). Thus, I can't fathom a way out of this disaster other than what I propose in this book. Also, our best economists and scientists must take their share of the blame for the predicament we find ourselves here in 2021, with national poor health, frightful social relationships and a plunging economy, as our government's report card. Considering the hidden cost of government and managing society that follows, not only compares us to China, as I did in the introduction, but the rest of the world that now is in an economic war, trying to avoid military takeovers and celebrate democracy fiscally and socially:

Chinese Communist Party (CCP, Inc. a low overhead very efficient competitor in the USA's economic, globalization war)

CCP, Inc. is the largest enterprise in the world. It has 98 subservient companies with 12 on the Fortune 500 list. It has 775 million proletariat workers with no say. It has a politburo board of directors with one President. It has no unions, no Articles of Incorporation. It has no by-laws or rule of law for accountability. It has no restraint of trade limitations or anti-trust law. It has no HR human relations department. Its only investor is a communist party politburo. It has only one stockholder with total veto power. It has no contract with its employees. It has no complaint department. It has no work ethics standards. It doesn't need efficiency experts. It has no required quality control. CCP, Inc. has a more efficient labor force without interference of human rights, unions and strikes. Yet in the background are the 350 million believers in Falun Gong who have opted out of the CCP and support human rights and free market capitalism. The next twenty years will decide if the USA will lead the world out of war and poverty by establishing Humanism and peaceful coexistence as United Nations' standard.

CCP, Inc's research and development is hacking and stealing secrets of others for its technology. It embeds its citizens in its competitors Universities and communities for stealing ideas and technical applications. It has no 50 Republic States to control or satisfy. It has investors from its competitors ... American union pension funds, foundations and group mutual funds are investing in stocks and bonds of CCP's subsidiary companies in a single economy (unwittingly American investors are investing in a communist regime to the tune of $400 billion dollars per year, one-third is from the USA government Treasuries, that will grow to $1 trillion in market value by the end of 2021). This creates a dichotomy with current international politics with the USA using sanctions, tariffs, that are anomalies when it comes to winning the globalization cold war ... the reverse of CCP investing in USA companies is closely controlled by the CCP, a monopsony and a monopoly (a one buyer and seller market that controls all trade agreements and enforcement of competitive influences). All this converts to low quality with little to no overhead for its subsidiary companies. Also, no strikes, no work stoppages, media attacks, no protests other than religious groups, compared to 40% fixed overhead to run USA enterprises.

CCP, Inc. taxes small to large companies 2.5 to 15% Individuals 3% to 45%, on worldwide income. Therefore, CCP, Inc. is low overhead and high return on investment. On the other hand, 59% of the CCP workers are over 50 years old with a mandated social security program. 90 million drop out of the work force per year. Of the 775 million workers 10% are over 70 with a 54 average retirement age. Chinese national health care covers 90% of its vast 1.4 billion population as a private and public partnership with a variety of options. It is not a free cover all policy.

CCP, Inc. follows a single standard time offset even though it spans five time zones and borders 14 countries in Asia. China is the fourth largest with 2.6 million square miles behind Russia's 6.6 million, Canada's 2.8 million and the USA 2.7 million square miles. With the USA and Canada leading with natural resources. China trails the USA in GDP with $14 trillion to the USA of $21 trillion. Japan is third with $5 trillion, Germany fourth with $4 India fifth with $3 trillion. From these recent analytical figures, the USA is leading in GDP from a work force of 169 enterprising Americans with the highest overhead costs and lowest return on investment compared to China ... that is catching up by controlling the supply lines with low labor costs and high technological theft.

CHINA A TROJAN HORSE RESIDING IN AMERICA

The Trojan Horse was the wooden horse used by the Greeks, during the Trojan War, to enter the city of Troy and win the war. Is the CCP, Inc. (Chinese Communist Party) currently residing in America as a Trojan Horse? How about the imbalance of trade with China of $80 billion per month and $400 billion per year? How about the $1.3 trillion we owe China for this imbalance? How about China's capitalizing on economies of scale for low labor and overhead costs dictating the supply lines for major American companies and our consumption driven free market enterprise? How about technology theft from embedded students in major universities and tech companies? How about 100 million Americans using Chinese video games 12 hours per day and 80 million using Tik Tok videos as a surveillance robotic source? How about the influence on American habits China has by using brain drain hacking the algorithms of data provided by Google, Facebook, Instagram for psychological warfare? How about China's ownership of 400,000 acres in Texas and other locations for constructing wind farms?

How about Chinese campaign funding of American politicians? How about the $40 billion contributed to American colleges and universities and infiltrating education with Confucius Institutes in the US? How about Chinese students first in STEM courses in their government-controlled education and the USA is 38th in Math out of 71 countries and 24th in science while the most expensive for less advancements in academic achievement? How about China's 77,000 PhD's produced per year compared to USA's 40,000? How about the 7.47 million immigration applications and 712 thousand green card applications with 20% being from Asia, submitted in 2020 with 56% approved? How about 90% of PPE, personal protective equipment, being produced in China to deal with the China Covid-19 virus released from the Chinese Wuhan lab?

Is this a conspiracy theory or facts that has "Washington Burning" Rome Style with the collapse of the American political system using a socialist manifesto devised by President Biden and his team of Harris, Pelosi, Schumer, Sanders and Warren for fulfilling the Marxist philosophy of President Obama and his father.

Yes China, a monopsony (a one buyer market: see my book The Monopsony Game, Xlibris 2014), is taking away America's sovereignty in multiple ways under its "Wolf Warrior" campaign to destroy USA democracy and command the worldwide economic, health care, banking and military technology by controlling the mineral components (copper, rare earth, manganese) for the digital and cyber production of semiconductor chips by Taiwan and the USA. This will provide China a monopoly (a one seller market) on chip components for electric autos, cell phones, military technology, space travel, satellites and robotics. In my Trilogy, The American Enterprise Party, the swing vote, I propose how we can win the ongoing Cold trade and technology War using the swing vote in Congress to focus on how to dismantle the China Trojan Horse.

The current problematic situation is being exposed by the new administration's policies for open borders (2 million illegals let in during a disastrous exit of Afghanistan and opening the southern and northern borders), stopping energy production by closing down the Keystone Pipeline, proposing $3.6 to 6.2 trillion dollars of deficit spending that requires thousands of billions of borrowing from China and taxation of every American. This transformation, using a conflict of interest of the Biden family, turns America into a subsidiary of the CCP, Inc., a cold war clone of Chinese communism. A true conspiracy.

THE DEPTH OF THE SWAMP IS DROWNING THE ENTERPRISE
(Reign in Big Brother and the Brotherhood)
(Some of this data is repetitive but necessary to motivate readers to vote for The American Enterprise Party)

US federal spending $6.6 trillion, deficit $4.4 trillion, recorded debt $28 trillion ($84,000 per citizen), Medicare $1.3 trillion, Medicaid $1.1 trillion, Defense $720 billion, Interest on debt $392 billion, Federal pensions $300 billion, Agriculture subsidies $205 billion, total State, Federal and local spending $10.1 trillion (percent of GDP 47%), US GDP $21.2 trillion, total workers' compensation $11.5 trillion, US Federal tax revenue $3.4 trillion, ($10,440 per citizens/$27,000 per taxpayer), tax revenue to GDP 15%, US spending to GDP 31%, tariff tax $70 billion, US trade deficit $867 billion, China $300 billion, US imported oil $100 billion,

Unstable Population of 330 million (up from 320 million in 2000 and increasing at the rate of one million per year), US work force 155 million, pre-pandemic, 18 million unemployed, post pandemic 40 million, self-employed 8 million, union workers 15 million, not in workforce 81 million, government employees 22.7 million ($1.2 trillion annual payroll plus full pensions funded by taxes),

Median home value $326,000, median income $35,000, manufacturing jobs 15 million, US veterans 18 million, US homeless 556,000, US armed forces 1.3 million, Medicare enrollees 77.6 million, Medicaid recipients 61.3 million, without insurance 35.8 million, living in poverty 29.5 million,

Total State revenue $2.1 trillion, local sales tax revenue $1.5 trillion, Federal revenue $3.4 total US revenue $7 trillion, property tax revenue $542 billion, State debt $1.2 trillion, States unfunded pension liability $6.2trillion, local debt $2.1 trillion,

US total debt $82.2 trillion ($248,000 per citizen, $961,000 per family) (public debt to GDP 1001%), US total interest paid yearly $3.8 trillion ($ 15,000 per adult), US bank revenue $841 billion, (savings per family $28,000), total personal debt $20.7 trillion, ($62,600 per citizen), mortgage debt $16.6 trillion ($209,000 per mortgage, student loan debt $1.7 trillion (438,000 per student), credit card debt $965 billion ($6,000 per holder),

Federal Reserve shareholder profits $81.9 billion, FR unfunded interest $53 billion, US monetary base $5.3 trillion, currency and credit derivatives $615.7 trillion, US treasury dollars $790.7 billion, lobbying money spent $3.6 billion, campaign money spent $7.3 billion,

The top 1% wealth $60.8 trillion, bottom50% wealth $1.8 trillion, small business assets $12.8 trillion, corporate assets $15.4 trillion, household assets $127 trillion,

Social security liability $20.9 trillion, Medicare liability $32.4 trillion, US unfunded and unrecorded liabilities $158.7 trillion ($479,000 per citizen) as of now.

On the web site there are debt clock reports worldwide by country, by each US state, by past and present Presidents. Also, the wealthiest individuals and companies in the USA. These alarming numbers are being tracked by the US Chamber of Commerce, for use in planning, with neither party dare to refer to them in budget hearings, budget passage, restraint on lawmaking, borrowing, cost of annual deficits, interest expense, and unsustainable redundant Federal and State agency costs at all levels of government. In other words, the two-party establishment system run by the gangs of 545 over the last 50 years is hiding the fact that they have bankrupted our future with no reasonable bailout plan. Until this book, there haven't been attempts to change the thinking of Americans, "that our two-party establishment system will never let us down or lead to destruction". But it is too late to say "it's a speed bump that can be overcome by America's will and faith in the American Dream", when the US Treasury fails to send out social security checks and Medicare payments.

Well, if you are of that thinking, you should reconsider where we are and where we're going over the next decade and millennium. Because we can't plan for everything including the poor health of our countrymen and women that is exacerbating the Pandemic of 2020. And the Pandemic is changing the way we live, the way we think, the way we vote and the way we will consider who will guide our economic and financial future. Following is an excerpt from my latest health care book "Health Care for All" (SHIFT the paradigm to a Public-Private partnership), Page Turner Press, January 2021

American Enterprise Saves America From Pandemic

When the Corona Virus emerged from the Wuhan Lab, China made its move by controlling the flow of masks, PPE and pharmaceuticals to the world. Panic ensued and America was swept into shortages of hospital beds, ventilators, masks PPE, without a vaccine to fight the war. President Trump the entrepreneur stepped up and closed the borders to international travel January 31, 2020, coordinated the production of ventilators, provision of hospital beds and started the 'Warp Speed" vaccine development May 16, 2020. American enterprise delivered by the end of the year in spite of the failure of the American bureaucracy to produce a vaccine in 100 years. While Dr. Fauci and the CDC said it couldn't happen that fast then wanted to take credit for the effort. American enterprise wins the war while the government failed to produce results for a Pandemic that they may have participated in its origin.

THE 2020 PANDEMIC overwhelmed the hospitals, nursing homes and the medical community that failed to separate Covid-19 patients and warn the (political) scientists of the problems in administering mass mitigation without risk analysis:

- Of the 591,000+ US deaths, 77,000 possibly preventable deaths in nursing homes with 22,080 cases and 2,612 deaths in assisted living and congregate housing for the elderly and infirm adding another 10,000 cases.
- 80% of Covid-19 deaths are in nursing homes, assisted living and congregate living centers.
- 99% recovery rate in the general public with current therapeutic medications.

- In hind sight, the scientific cure may be far worse than the shutdown of our ability to fight this or any virus with current medical therapeutics while we pursue a vaccine (s).

THE 2020 CHINA VIRUS PANDEMIC a catalyst to change: Why it has to be fixed!

- Must have a National Plan for Pandemics and funding aging America such as the Chicago 2015 pandemic response plan which was not followed by Dr. Fauci and the Pandemic Task Force.
- The CDC, FDA and Institute of Medicine along with the World Health Organization should lead the campaign for prevention of chronic diseases as the forefront of our health care programs along with algorithms that can predict the severity of the virus and who are the most vulnerable to the death rate and who are the likely people to have immunity.
- The 2020 mitigation tactics inherited from the 1918 pandemic are the worse approach to reducing the death rate and the bureaucracy's failed vaccine development. The use of enterprise by President Trump produced "warp speed" results thus saving millions of lives.
- Must discharge cases to the hospital on doctor's orders for virile pneumonia and Covid-19.
- Must not readmit cases to nursing homes, Covid-19 viral pneumonia patient until not infectious.
- Nursing Homes must be upgraded to handle ventilators (currently not allowed by regulations).
- Must have respiratory therapists on staff (expensive and not reimbursed directly).
- Must have adequate masks and PPE (patient protection equipment) (currently not reimbursed by Medicare directly).
- Must have negative air infiltration rooms (highly expensive and not reimbursed by Medicare directly).
- Must have daily physician rounds and 24/7 RN involvement (currently not reimbursed by Medicare directly).

Why we Must Fix HealthCare Funding!

Currently health care funding is a $4.2 trillion annual cost (add $9 trillion dollars with the pandemic), political football. Proposals from both parties are suspect since they aren't based on performance or outcome. Medicare for All, the Public Option, Obama Care, private insurance do not deal with prevention as a policy or have health preservation as an objective. It is treatment and medication driven.

It is estimated that the prescription drug business in America accounts for $600 billion to $900 billion per year (growing at the rate of 25% per year (just look at the dirge of pharmaceutical commercials pitching pills not prevention) in contributing to an overdosing society. (With supply lines controlled by outsourcing to China, USA was at the mercy of our own failure to foresee such an event).

With Children on Redlin, teenagers on opioid pain medications, midlife agers on opioids, statins and blood pressure meds, and old agers on oxycodone, hydrocodone, fentanyl, blood thinners, psycho tropics, blood pressure and cholesterol medications lowering life expectancy for the first time in history, not improving it, preserving it or preventing pandemics.

IMPACT ON AMERICA DUE TO THE 2020 PANDEMIC is catastrophic on the elderly and unhealthy Americans with the cure or vaccine was yet to be found since the 1918 Spanish Flu:

- Society is in a panic with political gamesmanship during an election year with China in the background as the perpetrator. Our Institute for Health headed by Dr. Fauci (that had partnered with the Wuhan Lab experiments on bats being the carrier), CDC, FDA weren't anticipating the severity of the air borne pathogen and failed to determine risk by age, location, airborne exposure and protective masks, PPE and personal responsibility.
- Health care providers over whelmed ... Hospitals and long-term care was not prepared for a pandemic. There were no approved therapeutics or vaccines available. Panic prevailed as our institutions stumbled.
- Hundreds of Thousands of businesses and schools closed down, some permanently. An agenda of fear has put our culture of courage on hold to follow unproven science. Eventually we must overcome this fear of fear itself using what we learn and win the war on our future.
- $6 to $9 trillion dollar loss in GNP, and increase in national and state debt with a loss of Federal and State tax revenues approaching $3 to 6 trillion dollars.

- Collateral damage to personal relationships and our culture of violence, vulgarity and excess wealth causing protests and uncivil riots.
- With scientists warning of spikes without solutions is not productive and exposes our public health bureaucracy as a part of the problem.
- Impact on Economy is yet to be determined with trade deficits climbing and 40,000,000 jobs being lost.
- Without removing restrictions on businesses and schools to be our first line of defense, the value of our currency and the resulting deficits and debt parallels insanity.

SOLUTIONS according to the CDC, FDA, Institute of Health and the World Health Organization we must stop the Americans' health decline that has damaged our herd immunity, life expectancy and quality of life that must be fixed:

- Manage any Pandemic with courage and qualified scientific procedures that include forecasting used by actuarial science and mathematical probabilities for risk analysis using AI to predict outcomes.
- Stop all international travel and close the borders when it is confirmed that a virus has reached the Pandemic level.
- The pursuit of a vaccine for Corona Viruses was announced by President Trump on May 20,2020 to be funded by the USA and parsed out to free enterprise pharmaceuticals who in "warp speed" produced the preventive and treatment vaccines predictably saving millions of lives worldwide.
- SELF-HEALTH standards must be established for Americans' lifestyles and remedies for the 2.4 million divorces per year (researches found married mates have better lifestyle habits due to fewer behavioral problems).
- Self-Health Insurance Funding Trusts for each employee to fund their own health care insurance and internalize the benefits for staying healthy.
- SHIFT the paradigm from government-controlled health care to private consumer-based health care for accountability and quality control.
- Amend Obama Care to (Affordable Care Act) incorporate consumer standards of quality and episodic artificial intelligence (AI) models for the pursuit of outcomes justifying provider incomes.

Centers of Disease Control and Prevention (CDC)

Advice Pertaining to Nursing Homes and the Corona Virus Pandemic.

Given their congregate nature and resident population served (e.g., older adults often with **underlying chronic medical conditions**), nursing home populations are at high risk of being affected by respiratory pathogens like COVID-19 and other pathogens, including multidrug resistant organisms (e.g., Carbapenems-producing organisms, CANDIDA AURIS). As demonstrated by the COVID-19 pandemic, a strong infection prevention and control (IPC) program is critical to protect both residents and healthcare personnel (HCP).

Commentary:

Per Epoch News: Based on data of U.S. deaths through August 23,2020 the new CDC handbook system counted 161,392 that were attributed to the virus. Using the older system, in effect for 17 years, it was 9,684. The difference was all deaths were counted regardless of underlying conditions that likely was the cause of death. Current data showed that there was an average of 2.6 underlying conditions for all 169,392 and only 6% of the deaths was the only cause for death.

Ironically, experiments conducted by the project titled "understanding the risk of Bat coronavirus Emergence" was funded by our own National Institute of Health, headed by Dr. Anthony Fauci; with $3.7million in USA government grants to the Wuhan Institute of Virology, suspected of somehow allowing the virus to spread throughout the world. Dr. Fauci, then headed up the Corona Virus task force that managed the Pandemic with questionable mitigation strategies throughout 2020 costing $3.9 trillion in 2020 and $1.9trillion in 2121.

Without the moves by then President Trump, that closed our borders to international travel January 31,2020 and started in May 16, 2020, "Warp Speed" development of multiple vaccines, millions more lives worldwide would have been lost. To his credit, he prevailed even though, he absorbed attacks from the left and right for not managing the Pandemic aggressively enough that ultimately cost him reelection.

September 16, 2020 New York Times

At least 77,000 residents and workers have died from the coronavirus at nursing homes and other long-term care facilities for older adults in the United States, according to a New York Times database. As of September 16, the virus has infected more than 479,000 people at some 19,000 facilities. Nursing home populations are at a high risk of being infected by — and dying from — the coronavirus, according to the Centers for Disease Control and Prevention. Covid-19, the disease caused by the coronavirus, is known to be particularly lethal to adults in their 60s and older who have underlying health conditions. And it can spread more easily through congregate facilities, where many people live in a confined environment and workers move from room to room. (While 7 percent of the country's cases have occurred in long-term care facilities, 200,000 deaths related to Covid-19 in these facilities account for about 40 percent of the country's pandemic fatalities.)

You Don't Know What You Don't Know
(Governor Cuomo errored then covered up the nursing home deaths)

While Governor Cuomo was building a following ranting that he needed 30,000 ventilators now! And 1,000 hospital beds he never used; he was forcing nursing homes to be the dumping ground for Covid-19 dying patients. Stupidly, he didn't seek counsel to find out that nursing homes aren't allowed by regulations to provide acute care. Any patient requiring hospital care for pneumonia, respiratory failure, high risk of stroke, heart failure, diabetic seizure, bariatric care for sever obesity must be transferred to an acute care hospital. And can't be sent back until stabilized. As a result, nursing homes don't have respiratory therapists on staff, aren't allowed to provide ventilator care since they don't have negative air filtration rooms, 24-hour on-site RN coverage and physicians making daily rounds for continuous supervision of Covid19 interventions, evaluations and treatment.

As a result, in New York over 15,000+ patients in nursing homes and hospitals expired due to the decision by Governor Cuomo to require hospitals to send patients with Covid-19 back to nursing homes and not accept readmissions of Covid-19 patients. Across the country nursing home patients were the highest risk group and highest death rate due to Coved-19. Unfortunately, other uniformed Democrat Governors followed Cuomo's lead using nursing homes as the dumping ground for overcrowded hospitals. This not only caused more deaths it exposed the other patients, the caregivers and their families to the deadly virus.

Ironically, by having his staff not accurately report the actual nursing home deaths, Governor Cuomo garnered a million-dollar book deal and an Emmy for exemplary performance during the worst of the Pandemic. Now, he may have to give it back since the truth has surfaced that he had his staff intentionally underreport nursing home patient deaths.

This was done, during the time that the democrats were blaming President Trump for mismanaging the Pandemic. While Dr. Anthony Fauci, our pro team President and the CDC were instilling a panic for the remainder of the year as Trump was dumped like the nursing home patients. Based on the task force being ill conceived or at best politically motivated, the Pandemic forced the closure of small businesses and essential schools without valid risk management. Their definition of essential businesses consisted of the Brotherhood Big Tech, Big Box, Big Media, Big Unions, Big Pharma Big Brother Government to stay open and never missed a paycheck while the rest of America was closed for months. The most damaging being our public school system where the Big Teachers' unions called the shots on not opening our schools to our children who had the lowest risk of transmitting or contacting the virus.

Granted my comments have some hindsight for my article published in August 2020 on Medium's website covered my research on the Pandemic that parallels current Fox News reporting regarding Dr. Fauci and his involvement with the Wuhan Lab. Also, Vice President Pence put together the task force and was ill advised to not have actuaries and medical experts as the managers not scientists who had failed to predict or mitigate the Pandemic for decades while Trump correctly blamed China and the World Health Organization as the coconspirators. It is now reported that Dr. Fauci and the Institute of Health funded experimental gain of function grants of $600,000 to $3.7 million to create a synthetic Covid virus that may have been the source of the release of the virus from the Wuhan, China lab into a worldwide Pandemic.

If this is true the $1.3 trillion owed to China for the $600 billion post Pandemic imbalance of trade per year, we should withhold payments until the $6 trillion cost of the Pandemic is repaid. Also, Dr. Fauci is going to have to explain why the cause of the Pandemic may be due to a human error in Wuhan lab and if USA was funding gain of function in a synthetic virus why was this not reported. His involvement in this scenario borders on a political conspiracy to blame President Trump for mishandling the Pandemic resulting in him losing the 2020 reelection.

The American EnterpriSe Party Platform

The structure of any American Enterprise (businesses) brings capitalism and socialism together pursing profits, standard of living, equal opportunity to attain the American Dream. So, why do we pit one against the other. The two establishment parties are labeled liberal versus conservative, Red versus Blue, capitalism versus socialism, racism versus all the other isms. Primarily, it's to justify bigger government and without accountability for our fiscal welfare, not just people welfare. Obviously, after the continuous 2020 election results and the end of the capitalist legacy of Donald J. Trump versus the coming socialism tenure of Joe Biden, America's two-party establishment politics has it all wrong. We need a third-party that, with a swing vote, can break up the marriage of the establishment parties that can't agree on anything. I repeat, it splits the independents away from the Democrats and the Republicans so neither has a majority. So, a third party does not assure any of the three parties a 51% majority allowing for the filibuster to really mean better legislation and laws.

The American Enterprise third party is dedicated to the American people who aren't racist, who feel unrepresented and unappreciated by the Gang of 545 (Senate, House, Supreme Court and the President) who now control our lives... it is not a wish, or a dream or a whim it is a culmination of experience and ideas that will stimulate discussions and change. In reading the American Enterprise party line please forgive me for repeating certain statistics, strategies and tactics. The context of the information is different but the repetitive relevant data, positive solutions and creative ideas are needed to make my case for shifting the paradigm from an oppressive establishment two-party system to a third-party alternative that represents enterprising Americans by reforming policies affecting governance of business, social, legal and world affairs.

Otherwise, the $158 trillion debt will have to be dissolved through a Chapter 10 bankruptcy process.

Preamble to the American Enterprise Party

We, the people of the United States of America, take back our sovereignty, and reclaim our right to have a say in the policies and conduct of our government. We are offering a third-party alternative for those enterprising Americans who pay for the public sector and do not currently have fair representation or input to the system that has caused many fiscal, social, and foreign-relation problems that face this nation of 313 million citizens and 24 million undocumented aliens.

The following initiatives are what this third party will pursue and enact under a more responsive and representative government.

We do not need entitlement reform. We need government reform. We currently have 22.7 million government employees, a one-trillion-dollar annual payroll, a twenty-five-trillion-dollar annual pension debt, and a 123-trillion-dollar accumulated deficit and a $158 trillion unrecorded obligations using GAAP. We will reduce the cost of regulations, not eliminate human-service programs. We will eliminate unionized pension plans and replace them with IRAs, or another form of personal pension withholding savings accounts that are *not* funded by taxes.

Any tax reform will eliminate taxes on adjusted taxable income and replace it with a flat 5 percent annual, five-year, assessment on individual and corporate net worth. The new entitlements, such as unemployment compensation, workers' comp, welfare, Obama Care, food stamps, paid leave, etc. are eroding our American work ethic and need to be replaced with real, private-sector jobs that create a true return on our gross national product.

Job creation will be stimulated by downsizing government (fixed overhead) and upsizing the marketing of the private sector ingenuity. Ridding the economy of 50 percent of the regulators lowers overhead and relieves the stifling impact it has on the creativity, technology, and product development of small businesses. *We will put the producers back to work and get the checkers out of the way.*

We will recapitalize the American enterprise by assessing 5 percent of the net worth of the wealthiest companies and individuals (some economists call this the wealth tax) to pay down the national debt to a manageable level. This will allow investors to make their own decisions and strategies without the infringement of government enforcers, and replacing debt instruments with equity from foundations and tax shelters for those who have profited from the great American enterprise.

Healthcare needs to be privatized based on an enterprise model where self-health funding shifts spending away from enforcement to pay for collaborative rules and regulations for self-health incentives. The unhealthy must be responsible for their own medical costs through a withholding program that is invested in mutual health insurance companies who will invest the reserves into small business that will share in the cost of health and fitness programs. Quotes from "Health Care for All" (How to fix nursing homes and prevent Pandemics) a book by Jerry Rhoads, published by Pager Turner Press, 2021.

Alan Greenspan said that "Social Security is not our problem, it is healthcare. Let the market demand dictate the distribution of dollars, not the Congress or the Fed". Of course his advice was ignored as Congress passed the biggest entitlement of them all . . .Obama Care.

Education also needs to be privatized, managed and funded at the local level (Charter Schools have proven this concept). It's the inner cities that are in trouble and need to be upgraded through sales taxes not property taxes. Slum landlords don't pay enough to property taxes to fund education. As the Pandemic has proven the Teachers Service Unions are not in sync with science nor local priorities. Our most valuable assets have been deprived of two years of their development due to the mismanagement of the Pandemic in our education system. The teachers should have been designated essential and required to stay open. Then along comes the 1619 project of reverse racism and CRT (critical race theory) compounded by the George Floyd uncivil riots being used to further the Black Lives Matter revolution calling white Americans systemic racists and supremacists. Further exacerbating the feud between public and private schooling.

FOR THE KEYNESIANS, PROGRESSIVES, ESPOUSING LIBERALS, CHANTING CONSERVATIVES, TEA PARTIERS, RELIGIOUS RIGHT AND TRICKLE DOWN ECONOMISTS, THE AMERICAN ENTERPRISE IS IN TROUBLE. . . THE AMERICAN DREAM DERIVATIVE BUBBLE WILL BURST WHILE THE RED AND THE BLUE CONGRESS AND ADMINISTRATION FIDDLE. ROME ALL OVER AGAIN.

American business should be the purchaser of last resort, not the government. The government is a service agency directed by the private sector's needs. No regulation is more important than the physical, fiscal, and social health of the nation. Otherwise, we have insured the demise of the great American enterprise. Robert Reich former Secretary of Labor for Clinton Administration was heard stating that the Government should be the purchaser of last resort and the CEO of Exxon stated, when asked about energy exploration, he stated his top priority was to make a profit ... both are condescending to the America Enterprise System that is to serve all of its citizens most of the time not its individual monopolies, monarchs and czars.

It comes down to would we rather have politics or money- tics. Politics is the art or science of influencing people on a civic or individual level, when there are two or more people involved. Money-tics is where you alter the term people and insert money before the people. When this becomes the culture terrorism, gun control, illegal immigration, health care, education is influenced by fear factors that are not an art but a science, because fear is always optional depending on its degree and likelihood of happening. Fear tactics are utilized, as Michael Creighton taught us in his book State of Fear, by vested interests to move their agenda into action. For example: Terrorism is the systematic use of fear, often violent, as a reason for coercion. Some of those tactics are utilized in this book for attention getting only. Any resulting coercion of our current public officials is up to the voters.

Update: The latest vestige of Fear being used as a strategy and tactic for controlling Americans was demonstrated in the Pandemic of 2020 and its aftermath. We allowed a task force of bureaucrats to scare the devil out of our very rights to congregate, do business, commingle with family, travel, go to the gym to be healthy, seek help for depression, make a living ... a so called cure worse than the Covid-19 Pandemic where no stratified data was used to bend the curve by age group, risk pools, underlying conditions ... just generalized useless tactics to slow and bend a generalized curve. Examples of mismanagement are emerging when we look back with 20/20 clarity that we were led by fear mongers not patriotic leaders. For example: Dr. Fauci and Governor Cuomo, media celebrities who ruled by fear and false positives not true negatives.

After 12 months of this tactic a vaccine was introduced as a possibility for herd immunity ... not by the scientist experts from the CDC, WHO, Institute of Health or government health agencies but by American Enterprise, and business man President who is then forced out of office by a suspect election with a new party inaugurated as the new savior. Meaning a change in establishment binary two-party polarization and log jammed response to a bloated government swamped with debt and impending stock market crash and depression due to escalating prices and collapse of the value of the American dollar ... now in the hands of progressives seeking the green new deal, forgiveness of collage debt and revamping of government as established by the constitution. I reiterate for the umpteenth time, more reasons for an effective third-party such as being herewith proposed.

Changing Government is inevitable so it does not change all of us into robots, drones or rebels. Our personal freedoms are on the line and I mean the battle line. Collectively, we have the right to fair and honorable representation . . . your vote counts so use it for American Enterprise.

Political Parties

"The failure of American politics to engage us in full is not an inherent weakness in the American system of government, only in the entrenched, political establishment that would have us believe we have no alternative to them. There's nothing in the Constitution that says, 'You will be divided into two main political parties, Democrats and Republicans, and together they will determine the direction of the country, even if that direction is into the ground.' Their shared dominance of our political system is merely a product of our own malaise. They're so big for no other reason than we've all played so small. Neither Democrats nor Republicans seem to see the writing on the wall; perhaps it is still written in invisible ink. Our political parties have abdicated the sacred trust we place in them and we are married to them in our minds no longer. They have undermined the moral authority of the American political system; we do not trust them anymore."

–*The Healing of America* by Marianne Williamson

An effective Third-Party Candidate may be part of the answer.

"I heard quite a few people speaking on TV before the last presidential election, unhappy neither candidate represented their highest hopes. And yet most Americans, even if there is a third-party candidate who more nearly expresses their views, are afraid to vote for that person lest the Democrat or Republican who most offends them might then win."

–The Healing of America by Marianne Williamson

Why would America now want a total revamp of the establishment two-party system? In the past the third-party candidates merely influence the outcome between the two-party establishment candidates and do not change the process. But now based on the following predictions for the progressive liberal Biden first term it may become self-evident that America is headed in the wrong direction:

Twelve steps to American bankruptcy:
1. Cooking the books (ignoring GAAP principles).
2. Excessive debt (debt exceeds GDP).
3. High interest rates (Federal Reserve causes recessions).
4. High unemployment (untrained legal immigrants).
5. Declining GDP (high prices, excessive taxes).
6. Declining stock Market (low productivity and morale).
7. Excessive government overhead (too many bureaucrats).
8. Fake news (media run by government of political parties).
9. Loss of Freedom of Speech (big tech, big government, big business control of government as a Monopsony).
10. Questionable election results (mass mail in votes without restrictions for indemnity and preregistration).
11. Gridlocked no consensus congress, legislatures and school boards (governing by committee not by enterprise). Replaces democracy with oligarchy control of a two-party system touting Capitalism and Socialism as extremists and opponents.
12. Culture of violence and vulgarity (Roman style).

Ben Stein in his article "Don't Fear Corporations" states, "Corporations in our era do not start wars, or crucify people, or send women and children to death camps. No, only governments that people who hate corporations love (usually because they are envious of the guts it takes to run a business and crave the security that government seems falsely to offer) commit atrocities. Corporations give us most of the good things we enjoy day by day in the way of material goods and services and do it in a usually effective, law-abiding way. The governments and politicians that go after them are the ones to fear."

John Stossel, in his book *No, They Can't: Why Government Fails but Individuals Succeed,* "government has become so bloated that practically every person in America is guilty of violating at least one of its arcane rules every day . . . the rules stem from the alphabet soup of government bureaucracy—IRS, DEA, EPA, OSHA, FTC, FDA—so government over regulation is what kills opportunity, not capitalism."

What Is Capitalism? Pe chicken or the Egg . . . **author unknown**

The best way I've found to justify capitalism is to compare it to other forms of socioeconomic and political systems. To do this, let's look at how the fruits of a chicken's labor are produced and disbursed under Nazism, Fascism, Socialism, Communism, and finally Capitalism.

Nazism: This is where the government commandeers the hen before the eggs are hatched and raises the offspring as a perfect line. Only the bad eggs are given to the people.

Fascism: This is where the government captures the eggs as they're laid, eats the yolk, and gives the shells to the people.

Socialism: This is where the people are given the hens. The eggs are laid according to the letter of the law and given to the people for one-half their wages in the form of Social Security taxes. The bad eggs are given back to the producers for recycling in accordance with environmental protection laws.

Communism: This is where the hens are owned by the government. The eggs are commandeered by the government for equal distribution to all. Only the average eggs are given to the people. The best eggs go to the politburo. The good eggs go to the Olympic team. If the annual quotas for production aren't met, the people are fed to the chickens.

Capitalism: This is where the people own the chickens. They buy the feed and risk their capital. The eggs are sold and the profits, if any, are taxed. The chickens are overworked and underpaid, but protected by unions. The unions guarantee collective bargaining, pensions, and equal opportunity for each and every chicken. The good eggs end up in the omelets served to the lawmakers, the bad eggs are chastised by Rush Limbaugh and called Fascists, Nazis, Socialists, and Communists.

In American parlance, we do not have perfect capitalism when we have the government purchasing 75 percent of everything. You have a monopsony (an oligarchy). When you put the government in charge of being the purchaser of last resort for anything, you have waste, loss of personal freedoms, misappropriation, and average to below average results. And our two-party establishment system has failed us with waste, mismanagement of taxation and spending without compunction and accountability.

The irony of this is in fact capitalism and socialism are bedfellows in our free market enterprise system. An enterprise (we call business) needs capital to function economically and people to manage the function of supply and demand … or in simpler terms capitalism and socialism are the components of humanism in the great American Enterprise that is the symbol of the American Dream. Not warring opponents on the field of play but identity labels used to confuse the voters when they want accountability before they choose their party … of course the capitalists want control of the money and the socialists want control of the decisions that affect their share of the money and profits. This is a war between the so-called "tax hating" conservatives and the "give away the shop" liberals when in fact they are like a waring family wanting to get their share of the business without working for it.

When in fact we need an arbitrator of the establishment factions that represents enterprising Americans who pay all the bills and taxes being the swing vote on how the business should function for all parties. Not a union but a free market entrepreneurial party that acts as a catalyst to the balance of power to run an efficient and effective economy with accountability and financial viability for all constituents.

The following is an illustration of the impact of being average: the guy has a bare foot in the bucket of ice-cold water and the other in a bucket of boiling hot water and on average he should feel great. But in reality, relegating everything to average is wasting away valuable resources on average to below average work ethic and guaranteed low quality.

In the final analysis, it's a question of which you would rather be: the chicken or the egg.

Our society has allowed the regulators to water down our standards by using the concept of minimum standards. We have left the definition of quality to the left and right side of the aisle.

On both sides you have the do-gooders, the defenders, the loyalists, the progressives from Harvard, Stanford, Yale, Georgetown law schools who dream of being a senator or president someday without regard to the constituency. Assuming power is the objective and money is the means to their end goal: having it all.

In the middle there is nothing other than 169 million enterprising but disgruntled workers without fair representation or a way to improve their earning power or chance at prosperity by losing ground to the elite and largess operators. With too many laws, regulatory impediments to enterprise, and jobs requiring skills that have been shipped overseas with the American worker on his/her way to being the servant, not the served.

During the past 45 years, each Congress has introduced an average of 11,000 bills. Out of those 11,000 bills, less than 5% actually became law. That is a 45-year total of 555,000 bills with 30,000 laws and thousands of pages of regulations and enforcement penalties.

January 1, 2010 was a big milestone in this scary look into the future with the introduction of 40,627 new bills were introduced (estimate for 2021, 40,000 plus again) and only 5% ever go into effect throughout the nation and its territories. That is 2,000 Federal laws per year with some 800 bills on average per state in the union, covering as widely diverse topics as texting while driving to mold removal in homes and criminal laws against people who scam other people. Each law must be funded and adds to the state and federal deficits at an astounding rate. It is killing the great American enterprise. President Biden is hell bent in increasing regulations and reversing the thousands that the Trump Administration took off the books.

Even though the stock market has almost tripled since 2007, the increases are primarily from investments into mutual funds of public monies for public pension plans and the Fed using the printing press to create a false currency in the form of US Treasuries. This continues to inflate the economy and devalues the dollar, plus the temporary investment of borrowed funds from foreign creditors goes into this deflationary cloud without making it down to small businesses.

What happened to the pursuit of excellence that we talked about in the '80s when Tom Peters highlighted American ingenuity and commitment to the progress of the working man and woman? In those days smaller was better but bigger was gaining momentum by outsourcing to other cheaper labor. Interestingly, if our government overhead was not 33 to 40 percent of GNP and the work ethic had not been destroyed by the new entitlements (unemployment and workers' comp, disability, unionized pensions for public servants, PTO, etc.) our labor costs would now be competitive with the benefit of hungry Chinese, Koreans, Mexicans, Japanese, Eastern Indians who now want their version of the American dream.

So, maybe the answers we are seeking and proposing in this book is to lower the 40% fixed overhead and let enterprise breathe, and decide the benefits for those employees who are above average and have earned their higher income. Rather than relegating everyone to a mediocre "everyone is the same" performance. "How can we be better if we all are the same?" Author

George Washington, the father of American Enterprise: "Government is not the reason. It is not eloquent; it is a force. Like fire, it is a dangerous servant and a fearful master."

The American Enterprise "needs a party for the underdog and appeals to the aspirations of the American people," *Newsmax* publisher Christopher Ruddy. The American Enterprise Party is the alternative that represents the enterprising nature of the majority of Americans, be they white, black, brown, red, or yellow; foreign, alien, or naturalized citizens who work and support the fearful master: a government burning out of control.

Adam Smith, father of capital deployment and Enterprise: *"The general industry of the society never can exceed what the capital of the society can employ.* Debt capital employed by society can be a friend to the needy and an archenemy of the republic."

- The Republic of the United 50 States, supreme power held by the citizens to vote and is exercised by elected officials and representative government according to Rule of law.
- A democracy: supreme power held by the citizens to vote and is exercised by elected officials and representative government according to law.
- An enterprise: undertaking challenge, readiness for daring action, a business model, organizes and assembles an enterprise for work, security, and happiness.
- A social enterprise: George Will is famous for saying "Americans want a welfare state but do not want to pay for it," that is the definition of the social enterprise that makes the government the benefactor but also the choke point for funding its commitments to the beneficiaries (See Exhibit C in Volume II) examples of the government committing fraud and abuse of the Medicare and Medicaid recipients).
- An American enterprise: the social and business model integrated by splitting the service agencies between the public sector and the private sector by downsizing government and upsizing business for the good of society. For example, using the Charter School model to shift the paradigm from public schools to private enterprise education.

- Free enterprise is a misnomer, meaning the free flow of supply and demand, but that assumes no restraint of trade or no government intervention, which is a pipe dream.

Are these different factions or bedfellows or a contradiction? As George Washington predicts, when one is pitted against the other, we have a dominant servant and a fearful master. So the time is to promote nationalism (devotion to national interests, unity and independence of thought and action) and patriotism (one that loves his or her country) for the good of the American Enterprise. It is a blending of the political process and economic realities to formulate a provocative but effective fiscal plan that brings socioeconomic politics to the majority not the selfish influence of the minority, for it is the majority that will fund the process and create a responsible balance for the future. Therefore, we need to deal with the real obstacles to taking back America from those that created the problems.

Enterprise Party (corporate by-laws, board of directors, and complete party platform presented in Chapter 13 Volume II)

- Offer a third alternative to the establishment binary two-party system that will focus on America's middle-class, aging population, legal immigrants, youth, and small business as a strong voting consensus that America must build on *peace* and *enterprise* not *money* and the *elite caste system*).
- Create private-sector jobs for reclaiming forests, repairing infrastructure, fighting, and preventing natural disasters (i.e., privatizing government jobs for America's response to natural energy creation).
- Devise a tax system that is based on net worth, not income or purchasing power (the death tax becomes a recapitalization of the enterprise, using wealth that is generated through the use of the enterprise for the standard of living for all enterprising Americans)
- Put individuals in charge of their own individual healthcare spending accounts to eliminate the middlemen (get government and insurance company overhead and profits out of the equation) who profit on illness, not wellness.

Divided we fall, together we stand. Let enterprising Americans have a role in governance due to the failure of the establishment two-party system to be accountable and effective in its leadership. We need leaders who allow the partnership between public and private enterprise solve the problems. Enterprise being the entity that brings monetary capital together with human capital to maximize return on America's investment in the health and welfare of the citizens of the Untied States of America. No longer will we have the fight of the capitalists and socialists destroy our democracy since both are drivers of the pursuit of the American Dream.

Causes of this failure:

Cooking the books cooks our goose: www.usdebtclock.org

Government ignores the very rules that enterprise has to abide by. Generally accepted accounting principles (GAAP) require that the debt for entitlements, pensions, and accounts payable that apply to a particular fiscal period must be recorded and matched to revenues that have been earned. Government being on the cash basis intentionally accelerates collections of taxes (paying in estimates for the next period's taxes) and defers expenditures as long as possible (unfunded but committed public-sector pension costs, Social Security pension costs, and healthcare costs) creating the illusion that we are better off than we really are. The $28 trillion debt is really $158 trillion if GAAP was practiced. Why are we allowing our elected officials to mislead us into thinking that we are not as bad off as we really are?

Cooking the economics with interest rates: www.usdebtclock.org

The Democratic Party blue economics: under "Keynesian" theory bigger government creates economic growth, cutting government spending hurts economic growth. Obama and his advisors are Keynesians. They believe that government spending creates infrastructure jobs and grows the economy; that using the Federal Reserve banking system to set exchange interest rates controls inflation and increasing taxes to balance the growth of the Federal budget controls the American economy.

The Republican Party red economics: under "trickle down" economic theory, increasing taxes hurts economic growth. Reagan and his advisors were trickle down advocates. They and current conservative

Republicans believe that cutting taxes creates jobs and grows the economy by giving entrepreneurs, small businesses, and risk-takers more capital to create jobs and grows the economy; however, in practice they promote continued growth of Big Brother government, and as a byproduct, want to cut acceptable entitlements and use lawmaking and punitive regulations to further control.

Cooling the debt and heating up the economy: www.usdebtclock.org

The American Enterprise Party economic formula: smaller government and elimination of the new entitlements induces profitable business enterprise by downsizing government, privatizing regulatory agencies, and economizing the cost of government creates the dynamics of enterprise, which are jobs, jobs, jobs, profits, taxable income, and GNP growth. Through reduced government overhead, capital development for infrastructure investment thrives, the deficits are eliminated, national debt is paid down and America's needed entitlements are intact.

The war on debt economics formula: mobilized workers, focused (Details covered in Volume 3) objectives, measurable goals, adequate financing for the duration, disciplined approach to work, flexible work hours, decks cleared of obstacles to mission (over regulation), measurable results. Examples, WWI and WWII created economic growth while the subsequent wars were not motivated by nationalism, because of the limitations put on the reason for the missions; i.e., no definable outcome and no resulting growth in income.

So, let's mobilize the constitution. Use the Enterprise structure, composition, and makeup of America to start a new form of government enterprise. Use the basic constitutional law in a socially organized third party. To do as the founding fathers pointed out, enterprise and capital are required, both human and monetary, so downsizing government, economizing natural resources, recapitalizing America's enterprise by using investment incentives; for those who have high net worth, to capitalize small businesses, entrepreneurial initiatives, and funding risk-takers is the essence of this book.

The real answers to great questions are below the obvious and above conventional wisdom. As Michael Crichton, in his bestselling book *Fear Factor*, said, "Conventional wisdom is invariably out of date. Because in the time it has taken to become conventional wisdom and become what everyone believes to be true, the world has moved on. Conventional wisdom is a remnant of the past."

Conventional wisdom and past experience demonstrate that a third political party cannot win—until now.

Ten reasons why we need an effective third-party alternative that is functional in controlling the runaway wasteful cost of government:

The existing binary two-party establishment oligarchy does not represent the 313 million American citizens and 30 million undocumented illegal immigrants many that could be imbedded by terrorists for later attacks. Just try to call up or on your "too busy to see you" senator or representative.

1. The red and the blue are not accountable to problem resolution, only their political disagreements on their selected social and fiscal issue, creating problems not solving them.
    a. Public servants have become public savants (savants may exhibit exceptional memory but have difficulty putting it to use. Savant skills are usually found in one or more of five major areas: art, musical abilities, calendar calculation, mathematics, and spatial skills).
    b. Private sector has become private slaves (taxpayers, workers, and common folks).
2. A "yes/no" answer has been lost and honesty disregarded.
3. The dollar means more than moral character.
4. Financial and moral responsibility to constituencies is not a requirement for being elected.
5. The term "lawmaker" commits us to laws we do not need and cannot afford. It dilutes our freedoms according to the constitutional right to due process. This destroys the creativity of the "job makers" and individual freedoms.
6. Our democracy has fallen to career politicians, unions, and bureaucrats. The reelection of incumbents that is currently 90% warrants term limits, 2 terms in the House and 3 in the Senate and no incest of relatives inheriting the seats.
7. Fair representation means more than the class system that progressive or conservative policies have relegated to enterprising Americans.
8. Public sector and service union dominance over monetary and tax policy dumbs down the enterprising private sector; i.e., Americans'

creative juices. The former public servants are now the ruling class.
9. The need for our public and private governance to stand up for the great American enterprise and the enterprising American's work ethic that is lost (see Volume 111 for how to restore it) in the oligarchy and the present socialized system.
10. The evolution of a social enterprise precedes socialism that evolves into Communism, where the Congress, Supreme court, and the administration become the politburo. After that is Marxism and all personal freedoms are forever lost unless we have another cultural American Revolution of 2026.

It comes down to pursuing positive solutions to negative externalities, as defined in *Super Freakonomics* by Steven Levitt and Stephen Dubner. What is an externality? "It's what happens when someone takes an action but someone else, without agreeing, pays some or all the costs of this action. An externality is an economic version of taxation without representation. The greenhouse gasses thought to be responsible for global warming are primarily externalities since each of us are generating some by-products we are not paying for." For example, if we are obese and don't pay for our healthcare costs, if we are retired, we are not paying for our health benefits, we are not internalizing the cost, and when we aren't compelled to pay the full cost of our actions, we have little incentive to change our behavior. "Today, people are being asked to change their behavior not out of self-interest, but rather out of selflessness."

"Not all externalities are negative." A positive externality is when we pay for public education and have no kids in school. That's why we have entitlements, to positively share in the cost of positive externalities. In their first book, *Freakonomics*, the authors establish that "moral incentives are the way we would like things to be and economic incentives are the way things are," so a third party political alternative is a needed economic incentive to have the common good internalize (fund through taxation) the positive entitlement externalities for the greater good of the American enterprise. But the taxation must be for that purpose, not the irrational expansion of the public sector.

Example: By having our own OPIC (Organization of Petroleum Importing Countries) as an intra-governmental first world control over demand can play a significant role in establishing the reasonable supply, demand and price of energy. It is imperative that we rethink our national energy exploration so off shore drilling and fracking for natural gas as our oil and gas extraction policy are not destroying our natural resources. At the same time, accepting we humans cannot manage the earth ... it will cleanse itself but we do need to conserve not chase pipe dream ideas for expensive and ineffective solutions (killing the Keystone pipeline and spending billions on wind when solar and nuclear methods are the future). Electric autos and solar panels not deprivation are the productive solutions. The use of smart farming and restoring the earth's natural use of carbons with the conservation of our forests and wet lands brings carbon dioxide back into the ecosystem and the good earth's reproductive system.

It is disturbing that fracking seems to be polluting our waters in the process of extracting natural gas supply. For automobiles to conserve energy consumption, being flex fuel capable (hybrids offering multiple options), will have to grow from 6% to 50% of the cars on the road and 50% of home usage provided by solar and nuclear or natural gas. Unfortunately, the bureaucracy tends to chase solutions without the involvement of the private sector. It is more money-tics than practical solutions that continue to bring us down to long range failure. Inventing ear marks to add to infrastructure financing of a $100 trillion pipe dream muddies the water as to what the American Dream needs, not what the progressive activist want.

Qualifications to write about solving negative externalities:

Why am I qualified to write this book on American enterprise and work ethics? I am not a professor of economics, not a PhD of any kind, not a politician, not an artist, not a bureaucrat, just a CPA-licensed entrepreneur that has struggled my whole business life working on ideas and pursuing my own enterprise against all odds. What are the odds; 60,000 new businesses are formed in America each month and about the same number go bankrupt each month. I was told by someone that said I should not start a business, that if you survive five years you have beaten the national average for small businesses. Well, I have survived in my own businesses for thirty-six years (1977 to now) and still doing it. Most, if not all, of that time was on inadequate capitalization and pursuing ideas that were definitely not main stream. To me that is what democracy and freedom to fail are all about.

Why would I ever start if the odds were so high? Well, I was fired by my boss and had no other choice than to pursue ideas that my boss did not buy into. So I started a business out of thin air and have been out of breath ever since. However, I have done it my way, as the song says it best. The path has been hard but gratifying as it continues to move upward to my personal agenda. My objective is to attain change in healthcare and my goals are to provide the elderly a better quality of life. Or is it goals and objectives? In my parlance, the objective is ethical work, and the goals are quality of work.

My first clue that I am by nature a salesman was being in the Lion's Club and selling more candy for the blind than anyone else by eliciting kids to approach adults for the sale and then providing the kids with candy. I became the rainmaker in the accounting firms I worked for and finally found out I was good at getting people to believe in me and my message. Having been somewhat introverted and shy as a child, growing up this inspired me to spread my wings. In my experience, the most important quality to be an entrepreneur is to be able to sell your ideas to someone else, but the idea must come from a proven ability to work it into that customer's profitable **enterprise**.

In the accounting firms, I was recognized as a Medicare expert from my background with a much larger accounting firm. In this role I was selling my ideas on how Medicare can benefit the elderly, and to this day that is my gig. I mustered out of one firm due to my desire to work for a larger firm and then got fired from that firm because I was too radical with my ideas of how to develop and grow the healthcare practice. So in desperation I started my own enterprise, an accounting firm (J. L. Rhoads & Co.) in my kitchen. From there my clients' needs dictated getting into software development, management consulting, management services, tax services, accounting services, and systems design and implementation.

I became politically involved as a recognized expert by trade associations and the legislators, testifying and crafting white papers for Medicare and Medicaid payment systems. This was all focused on the burgeoning healthcare industry, leading me into eventually owning and operating them; giving rise to six books on self-health and this book, a public declaration of intentions, motives, and views (manifesto) on America's fiscal responsibility and the need for more effective leadership in healthcare and the wealth care of a nation underwater.

The rest of the story. Michael Creighton, bestselling author, wrote in his book entitled *State of Fear* that fear is used as tactic for forcing political agendas on the masses. For example: use of the fear of global warming by the conservationists to propose deprivation rather than rational solutions. The "inconvenient proof" should be left to the scientists not Al Gore and his political agenda. In the best-selling novel by Yann Martel, a magical adventure story centering on Pi Patel, the precocious son of a zookeeper, states that fear is the only thing fatal to life. So, fear is used incessantly by politicians, bureaucrats, and media to make us comply with their initiatives, opinions, and issues; all the while distracting us from the reality of fairness and practical solutions:

For example (as proposed in detail in Volume I): conventional knowledge says our negative financial condition is caused by unfunded entitlements, so we have to stop our spending spree on these fixed costs even though we will hurt the aged and disabled. This abstract thinking is forgetting what is right and wrong. First of all, Social Security and Medicare trust funds do not belong to the government, though $700 billion has been borrowed to fight wars, and Medicaid is a safety net paid for by the taxpayers for needed health care. These are trust funds belonging to the beneficiaries. To deprive them of entitled benefits is illegal and should not be touched for the reasons they are being dissipated: loans to the general fund, purchase of treasury notes, payment of interest on national debt, rationing of the funds for care to others, payment for wars, etc. We do not have the legal right to impound these entitlements. We don't need entitlement reform; we need government reform.

For example (as proposed in detail in Volumes II and III): we need and can reduce spending on the **new entitlements** (Obama Care, unemployment, workers' comp, welfare, food stamps, public pensions, disability, work leave, COBRA, reparation, etc.) and trillions of dollars spent on stimulus and progressive ideology that have been entrusted to the government. They are diluting the work ethic and forcing businesses to pay expenses that are not related to producing products, profits, and taxes. Government and enterprise should be funding these entitlements out of increases in the GNP and GDP, if at all.

LAST WORD OF WHY WE NEED A THIRD PARTY

Taking on this mountainous task of justifying an effective third party to the voters, that started in 1991 out of frustration with both parties, is overwhelming when everyone I pitch it to says it will never happen. Never also applies to the Pandemic of 2020 and the election of a new President that defies all logic and common sense by ignoring the depth of the swamp and the eminent danger to not drain it to an affordable level. Otherwise, in my opinion, we become a version of the 1984 George Orwell warned us of in his book in 1945.

So, the bottom line of Volume I is to educate the voters on the depth of the swamp and about the reign of Big Brother government and who is the Brotherhood, while the political consultants tell the candidates "Don't try to educate the voter, let them blindly follow, not think they can tell you what to do". The other factor, of "why we have to do it", is even more important. That is the strategy, plans and tactics being activated by China. The Chinese Communist Party (CCP) is our opponent and is the Communist Marxist Manifesto "destroy Capitalism for the sake of a socialist benevolent politburo" that turns into a few controlling the many with fear and destruction of human rights and values.

I am, by nature, a poet so I have used poems to express my feelings to broaden the use of humanism as a platform and to explain why diversity is America, not a racist version of China or Russia. According to Aristotle's book on Poetics and Poetic Justice "there are three forms of governing bodies, a monarchy, a tyranny or a democracy". He adds, "poetry speaks more of what is universally the case, whereas history speaks of particular events." Those opposing philosophies that are wanting to cancel our history of pursuing peace and worldwide coexistence are not sustaining democracy but demanding their form of tyrannical control using fear and malfeasance. Whether we call them progressive or Red or Blue the intent is the same ... control of our national resources and economic powerhouse called American Enterprise. That is why millions around the world have and are coming to our borders to have a chance at freedom of opportunity and a peaceful, happy family life.

The following poems are expressing my feelings of freedom of speech to explain why humanism is way beyond racism, wokeism, capitalism, socialism or any other ism. As a reader and voter, you can disagree with my pentameter but the logic has an element of common sense that seems to have been lost in the protests and riots because of perceived systemic racism that alleges that white versus black (brown, tan, etc.) is worthy of a French type revolution. They are missing the point ... read the following poem "My (Our) America" before you pick one side or the other. Because together we stand and identity revolution tears us apart. If you believe I'm right please vote for the American Enterprise Party swing vote and read Volumes II and III for the full platform of "how to do it" and "who will do it".

MY AMERICA THE BOUNTIFUL

By Jerry Rhoads published in "The Eighth Wonder of the World"

My America is the feeling of freedom. It's the feeling good when you get up in the morning and can decide what you're going to do that day, who you're going to see, and what you're going to say.

It's the feeling that you can make a difference. It's the feeling you can produce your product, you can sell your produce, and you can benefit from your hard work, unhindered.

It's the feeling when you help your children with their homework so they will be able to use their knowledge for growth, for maturity, for the good of the country.

It's the feeling when you send them off to school, knowing they will receive a concerned teacher's attention, sensitivity, and guidance. And knowing as they grow up, they will thrive on their freedom to communicate, to express themselves, to direct their own destiny.

It's the feeling when they graduate from grade school, junior high, and high school that they are taking the steps toward a better life. And when you give their hand away in matrimony, that happiness shall be theirs. For together as husband and wife, they can create the same and even more opportunities for their offspring.

It's that feeling when you can unchain your dog and watch her run free for at least a little while, to watch the expression on her face when she's released from the shackles and the sadness that reappears when she must be chained.

It's the feeling of being in good health, happy with my spouse, with a family as my wealth; as My America is the opportunity to pursue such prosperity unbridled and unfettered.

My America is the freedom of choice to buy the bread I want to buy, to acquire the goods I can afford to acquire, to invest the capital I have saved in ventures I want to take for the love of my family and my country.

My America is being able to communicate in writing, speaking, and in whatever form, language takes, my opinions, my thoughts, my prayers, my visions, and my dreams to those who want to listen and to those enemies of the American way who in themselves have not discovered America.

My America is the blooming rose that has the freedom to grow toward a clear sky and a warm sun, being able to complete its cycle from bloom to plumage to autumn to a dormant grave, only to rise again.

My America is the personal commitment to grab opportunities that will better the country and to set an example for those who follow; what you give must be proportionate to what you take, or the erosion shall remove the sky, the sun, the earth from our grasp. For in our America and the world resources are limited; the energy, though absolute, is redistributed by our wills. The more astute, the freer we are to create, the better the use of the resources. And left in God's hands, through our America, we create good will, good products, good people, and peace of mind.

My America the bountiful, oh yes, my America, the vision of the poet, the words of the orator, and the minds of the leaders be kind, be patient, be wise, but above all be humble to the reasons and the heritage of our freedom. Lead us not into temptation, but deliver us from evil ventures and purposes, for thine is mine America as the Kingdom, the power, and the glory, forever.

Amen.

VISIONS OF A BETTER WORLD

("Tear down that wall" of violence, vulgarity and excess)

Look toward the sky of tomorrow
Feast on the setting sun
Let us look for less sorrow
Swear only if tyranny is undone

Dream not for the dying
But cherish the fruit of the living
With eyes not shut to crying
Put forth with open giving

Find and seek the soldier
To which the vision of a better world
Is in the heart of the beholder
With a democracy's flag unfurled

As monarchs and politicians loses sight of the practical
Common sense must prevail
If the common man is to scale obstacles
To a better version of the grander scale

Yet, thus a third party will be formed
With its principles of practical economics
As the answer and course the elite has scorned
Revitalization of enterprise must be the fix

With fewer divorces
Less crime and violence
Fewer military forces
More common sense

Higher employment
Better GNP and fun
Lower drug decent
Less people on the run

Better standard of living
Lower teen pregnancies

More charity and giving
More human decencies

More affordable housing
Fewer unwanted children
Less carousing
And immoral sin

Effective protests for change
Fewer uncivil riots for revenge
Less excessive income
More equality of outcome

Clean up our intercity
With equal opportunity
No inequality in education
With peace in our nation

Fewer weapons on the streets
More productive gangs
No inhuman defeats
Freedom to speak of better it brings

With Visions of a Better World
(A nonviolent loving culture with peaceful coexistence)

Yes, my vision of a peaceful world is
In the heart of a mother's decency
And the hope of individuals
Not in the theory and hypocrisy

Of the institutional intellectuals
Condemning us to mediocrity
This vision is what I call Mancology
The science of harvesting human values

In an enterprising theology
Outside religion and the pews
Vitalize our enterprise psychology
Let the established institutions redirect their energies

Into the livelihood of hard work, family life,
For the love of our fellow man's synergies
Embodied in man and wife
Replacing the negative forces hurled

With positive entities
And opportunities of a better world
Pursuing peaceful infantries
That don't stand down to religious fantasies

The skeptic forces of the self-righteous
Who must learn to work ethically
With a common cause and crisis
Though besieged by indifference ethnically

Will enact the vision that freedom unfurled
Under one flag one spoken word and a peaceful jihad
To become a better world
So help us God

So, governed of the people for the people by the people

PEACE ON EARTH

Peace on earth isn't likely to be free
To enforce our global sovereignty
Until we are attacked by an alien force

Racism and unrest of the masses
Creating castes and classes
Fail to bring us together
Leading to wars sins of commission and omission
As thunder doesn't stop stormy weather
When humanity forgets the mission

Peace on earth good will to men
That is peace, relations, cooperation, salvation of earth
Starting with the newest birth
And the oldest human's worth
Days don't end and nights become fears
When the past tense
Becomes the lack of common sense

We are a victim of ourselves
When we allow our culture
To degrade the importance of peace
Without arms, warriors and torture
Unless an alien landing
Grows into a conflict of misunderstanding
That the very worth of our earth
Has to enforce peace war not withstanding

That peace is a function of right not might

EQUALITY

The allegory that we are all born equal
Is puzzling since we are all different

Man is born to be equal
Not born equal
Not white not black
Not yellow not tan
Or red
It is only skin instead

Woman is born to be equal
Not born a man
Not born rough
Not tough
Not strong enough
Or gruff
It is only what is within her skin

So race or women take heed
Hear your calling
But remember your breed
We cannot have mares
Without the steed
And night mares
Without God's speed
In color and creed

Equality is only in the mind
Of the beholder
And by design
We all are getting older
And when it is time
To hear the bell chime
Being equal isn't worth a dime
It is the justice not the crime
It is the opportunity that is free

That makes the man and woman
and race equally
Sublime

BORN TO BE EQUALLY FREE

What's equality any way ...
I thought born to be free was God's will
And we are free to pursue our pay
Though life may be a bitter pill
Just to be equal

How can you divide human capital
Into equal pieces for all
And receive more from the same
Who don't multiply or add to the game

Though you may be bright
Come on don't you see the light
We're all not to have the same
Life isn't a silly ballgame

Profits are only the score
The bottom line is just numbers
Even the thief and poor
Have to count up their blunders

Profit have you ever tried to stop it
Have you ever tried to say its
It's no good kill it
Have you ever tried to burn petrified wood

Profit many people do try to stop it
They put it down
They say it's no good
To be happier than anyone should

For everybody should be the same
Take those goals away from the game
And hand out everybody their share
Shame... don't you dare

When your brother is going downhill
Even though he doesn't have any will

That it isn't fair
Don't you care

He didn't have the same chance you did
You lucky kid
Just because you worked hard
And your butt is scarred

Doesn't mean you should have more than your brother
More beans means you don't love another
More profit means you're happier than him
That makes his prospects slim

We've got to do away with have and the have nots
The aspiration and the drawing of lots
We've got to be a great society
We've got to exemplify parity

And split up the earth's blackest sod
Then when nothing seems to fit
Under the guise of the wish of God
We'll decide to again pursue profit

Among all us children of God
Tear down that dirty word
Called profit
The only profit we want
Is the one that expounds the ideology
Of total equality

For we were born FREE
And to be equal shall be the sequel
To the destruction of profit
Stop it and we all then shall be equal

We all shall seek the same level
Into the doldrums of mediocracy
Our routes shall take the same bevel
Into the bowels of untrue democracy

Volume I: The Swing Vote to Drain the Swamp and Reign in Big Brother and the Brotherhood

Into the waste of what used to be
Profit sure you can stop it
You could kill it
You can un-will it

But for such an act begs
And we will pay the price with bites
Even the dogs will stand on their hind legs
And ask for equal rights

For we are all born free
And to be equal
We must celebrate the death of profit
And the day that profit is dead

Paint us all a communist red

So don't you dare say ifs and buts
That with the opportunity to be equal
Only BIRTH warrants results
And acknowledge we are born free for each meal

When freedom and opportunity are the gradient
And effort is the quotient of what's real
Equality and the right to be free the intent
So give me liberty to be equal

What makes America great
Is it individual creative endeavors
With the good grace of fate
And dealing with multiple flavors

Or equality is the merit of learning
The pursuit of earning
By taking a chance
Capitalizing on life's romance

All a result of unequal effort
With unequal talent
With equal opportunities pursued

With equal dissent
With unequal profit earning every cent

How can you divide the capital
Into equal pieces for all
And receive more from the same
Who don't multiply or add to the game

Profits are principles of freedom
We are born free to fail
We are born free to overcome
Nothing else is totally equal

Wealth pursued shall multiply
Wealth shared equally soon disappears
Without me being me
Born free profitably

Any other world won't be equally free

PARITY

*"The state or condition of being equal
especially regarding status or pay"*

*The creation of man
Yea is it to equality
Or yea is it to opportunity
Is man created equal
Or were they created to be equal*

*Even babies are different
In size color in personality
So why does this make us equal
At birth and till we die*

*We aren't and never will be equal.
Equal rights and opportunity
Not hands-tying
For lack of trying*

*Is parity a democracy or a social ideology
Do the scales need to be balanced or are they fair
When in balance with nature
And when in receipt of effort
The scales tip to those who put forth
And tip the scales their way*

*Parity a road to equality
Or the epitaph of dichotomy
Only the perceptive shall see
And only the seeing shall perceive
That even time favors the purveyor of the work
That even heaven beckons those who shall not shirk
Their duties and good graces
Through industry health and good judgment*

*Yes it tis the purpose for clarity
To define and expose parity
As the Satan of society*

As the downfall of Houdini
And the ego of Mussolini
Give us parity

Or give us give us give us give us
But in all sincerity
Only the doers shall believe
Only the unlike shall conceive
And the successes achieve
Only the humble shall receive

That parity is only a means to deceive
Our match maker who is neither Jew or Quacker

THE RIGHT TO CHOOSE

When I think of my children
It brings the word amazing to mind
On the other hand I had no band of brothers
So my grandchildren get the label awesome
And Great Grandchildren fantastic
Making more than a bond of mothers and fathers

It's amazing what people do to themselves
While it's just as easy or hard
What people can do for themselves
Such is the enigma of the devil's
Or the Savior's wish

Why will anyone choose the devil's wish
Pleasure at the sake of self-respect
Health happiness and life itself
When they can have the Savior's wish
Peace for the sake of self-respect
Health happiness and eternal life itself

It's amazing we all must choose for or against ourselves
And some choose to do themselves in with sin
While others forsake urges and fortify
Themselves with love for family to supply

Amazing Awesome Fantastic moves
For this is life itself ... to win or lose
We are born to be equal
Just because of the way we choose
And the rules we don't abuse

SELF-ESTEEM

Peace and equality is a state not a condition

We all stand in awe
Of being special
Being different

Many strive to stand out
And end up the same
As the crowd influence is spent

Yes they're all the same
Trying to be different
Ending up misspent

Punk cool stoned
Chasing the same dream
I'm doing it my way

With self-esteem
Built on a loving dream
That we all can have peace
As long as hope doesn't cease

Warlords and dictators
Resist the force of freedom
But the people are the instigators
If they don't standup for self-esteem

If those who are imprisoned
Rise up on their back legs
And over throw what they've dissented
Waiting for destiny that fear begs

No amount of our country's
Desire to rehabilitate
History's fate
Futile esteem shall not dictate

*As peace awaits for all people
Who are standing with self-esteem
Peacefully this will redeem
The haters and warriors of futile esteem*

Ignoring the ways they scheme

STAND UP

It is said "Stand for something
Or you will fall for anything"

Stand up and be heard
But make sure before you retort
That you put substance in your word
Don't throw yourself upon the mercy of the court

Where they shall show you no mercy
If your point is merely to criticize
Downsize and or abort
What it's already the political retort

The world is in need of leaders
To direct its progress
Not just to satisfy the ire of the history readers
With the least amount of stress

So if you intend to stand up and shout
Above the mingling crowd
And your mind is prepared for the bout
Make sure your voice is loud

It takes courage to face a crowd
That can cast a stone
As you stand up proud
You'll feel as if you're all alone

Stand up don't fall as a shallow prince
But if you're willing to take on the bigger task
The rewards are many due to the suspense
And your answers must be to the questions asked

By not deceiving the clamoring crowd
Be accepted for what you know as truth
Don't present what you haven't vowed
Because seeing the vision is hard despite blue tooth

Shouting your voice is loud
Standing on your pulpit
You're said to be endowed
Not falling for something counterfeit

Standing on principle and substance
Your foundation is strong
And you'll only get the chance once
To fight for right over wrong

When you have established a following
Then the standing for something
Is a note you will have to sing
With every message you bring

And not fall out of favor because
Of feeling you know everything

AUTHOR'S BIO

Jerry L. Rhoads, the author, founder, and CEO of the American Enterprise Party has extensive experience in all facets of health care. He was a consultant who helped implement Medicare and Medicaid in hospitals, clinics, nursing homes, and long-term care campuses. He was licensed as a Nursing Home Administrator in multiple states and has managed urban, suburban, and rural healthcare facilities. He is a CPA and a graduate of Simpson College, in Iowa. He, his wife, and his son owned two skilled nursing facilities in Iowa and one in Arkansas. He has invented, with the help of his son, Artificial Intelligence (AI) software for managing the restorative processes for the elderly so they can be returned to the community. The author has also been a consultant to State and Federal Governments for devising payment methods for health care providers served on numerous committees developing legislation for long-term care and testified before legislative committees as an expert witness.

My entrepreneurial and governmental experience with expertise is in the following business models:

wife of 65 years. line 2 Vote American politics. The author has worked for a large public accounting firm, been a partner in two others, and has owned and successfully run his own businesses for 37 years. During that time, he started a CPA firm specializing in health care and added management consulting and software development to the services offered principally to nursing homes and small hospitals. Over the years his expertise in Medicare and Medicaid led him to represent long-term care Association members in proposed legislation and quality improvement methods for the operators of those small businesses.

He has written extensively and presented seminars and national workshops in 22 different states. He has six books published on the subject that he terms Self-Health books, proposing that the solution to funding America's declining health and escalating cost is to have each individual be responsible for making their own health and welfare decisions. By using funds set aside for them in investment withholding accounts they can make their own decisions in preserving their health while preventing chronic diseases that currently rage nationwide. Of course, without a better method than Obama or Biden Care, funding the health care benefits for 77 million baby boomers will result in rationing their benefits to younger populations and therefore, the elderly will not receive their entitled Medicare benefits they've paid for.

Jerry and Shari his wife of 61 years now live in Chicago, Illinois after being displaced to Iowa from 2009 to 2015 reversing their culture shock back to Iowa and Arkansas to run their three skilled nursing homes (small businesses) with their son. In their 70's they started a new business of restoring the elderly and disabled back to their homes. . . a new version of nursing home care termed Restorative Care. After seven years of fighting with the regulators over how their All-American Care restorative model positively changed the environment and quality of life for their patients, they sold them and they were turned back into warehouses by corporate chain operators.

They have four grown children, twelve grandchildren and five great grandsons and four great granddaughters so far. Jerry and Shari believe that middle America is and has been by far the greatest place to live after having consulted with nursing homes in 22 different states dealing with the most regulated business of all time . . . nursing homes. It is their mission, through this book and his other health care books, to change the punitive and negative disincentives that exist in the Federal and State survey process to a reinforcement approach that allows the small businesses to direct their own version of quality of life not just bureaucratic, arbitrary and capricious interpretations of the quality of care.

This will require that the payment methods also be changed to performance-based reimbursement (**Volume II, Exhibit D**) using add-on programs and quality incentives utilized by the state of Illinois in the 1980's that Jerry helped design and implement. For complete coverage of this proposal refer to Jerry's book "Health Care of All" (How to Fix Nursing Homes and Prevent Pandemics) published by Page Turner Press, 2021.

- Google Search engine.
- Wikipedia search engine.
- Orlando Sentinel 2011 article by Charles Reese "Who is the gang of 545 vs. 330,000,000 People (100 Senators, 435 Congressmen, 9 Supreme Court Justices and 1 President)".
- Affordable Care Act signed into law March 23, 2010 (Obama Care).
- Medicare regulations.
- George Orwell books ("1984" and "Animal Farm").
- Adam Smith book "Wealth of Nations".
- Aldous Huxley book "A Brave New World".
- US Constitution citations.
- Epoch Times reports regarding China.
- Dennis Prager quote.
- Jerry Rhoads podcast "American Enterprise Manifesto" 2020-21.
- Jerry Rhoads poems, books and articles.
- Margaret Thatcher quotes.
- Ronald Regan quotes.
- John Lennon lyrics.
- www.usdebtclock.org.
- www.americanenterprisepoliticalparty.org.
- Lee Drutman article for the National Constitution Center "Breaking the Two-Party Doom Loop: The Case for Multiparty Democracy in America" January 2, 2020.
- Linda Killian, book "The Swing Vote", St. Martin's Press, 2011.
- China's Economic Council long and short-term plans.
- Center of Disease Control quote 2020.
- Federal Disease Administration.
- New York Times quotes September 16. 2020 and June 16, 2021.
- Governor Cuomo quotes.
- "American Enterprise Manifesto" book published by Xlibris 2012, author Jerry Rhoads.
- "Health Care for All" book published by Page Turner Press 2021 author Jerry Rhoads.
- USA government budgetary information and statistics.
- Marianne Williamson, author of book "The Healing of America"
- John Streusel quotes.

- Karl Marx German Philosopher and author of "Communist Manifesto", 1843.
- Be Stein quotes.
- President Biden's Executive Orders, 2021 (Volume II, Exhibit A).
- Former President Donald Trump quotes.

JERRY L. RHOADS, CPA, GOVERNMENTAL CONSULTANT

My expertise is in the following business models:

CPA firms, Software developer, Management consulting in long term care, Nursing Home Management, Skilled Nursing Home ownership, Published Author in genres of health care, costing long term care, poetry, novelist, Self-Health, Self-Help, a political third party.
Companies: All-American Care, J.L. Rhoads & Co., CPA firm, Rhoads HealthCare Consulting, Management and ownership, Word Data Processing, software developer, Rhoads Limited Partnership, a tax shelter partnership, MBO Management By Objectives, Cost Report Consulting, ROSE Rhoads Offers System Excellence Profession Group, ROSE Systems, Inc., Rhoads Offers Systems Excellence, MRT Maximum Reimbursement Technology, ROSE Systems implementation.

Founder and CEO of the www.AmericanEnterprisePoliticalParty.org, a third political party, representing a swing vote in America can politics. Supported by Mr. Rhoads' American Enterprise Party Trilogy. Volume one why a Swing Vote for Humanism, Volume two Enterprise Manifesto, how to Keep America Great, Volume three, Restore the patriotic, and ethical world ethic.

You can find him via Spotify as a podcaster, The American Enterprise Swing Vote Party, his blogs with the same link, www.jerryrhoadsauthor.com, www.allamericanpoliticalparty.org. www.lifestylesforaging.com presenting a memoir with his wife of 64 years. jerry.l.rhoads@gmail.com.
BOOK TITLES AUTHORED BY JERRY RHOADS (Available in book stores, www.jerryrhoadsauthor.com, and on Amazon.com):

Health Care for All (How to Fix Nursing Homes, and Prevent Pandemics)\(a self-health book).
How to Stay Married Forever After (12 vows/habits to live b, :forever after)(a self-health book).
Life Styles (Of the Healthy, Happy, and Prosperous)(a self-health book).
Never Too Old to Live (a self-health book.
America in the Red Zone (a self-health book).
Restore Elder Pride (a self-health book).
Remedy Eldercide (a self-health book).
The Monopsony Game (an economic analysis).
Failing Government Taketh Away (a political analysis) .
American Enterprise Manifesto (a third political party proposal).
Basic Accounting and Budgeting for Long Term Care Facilities.
Americana 2184 (a novel revisiting George Orwell's 1984).
Human Cology (the science of managing human value).
Cost Accounting for Long term care facilities.
The Eighth Wonder of the World (our amazing human eternal mind).
The Ninth Wonder of the World (our amazing human eternal brain).
The Tenth Wonder of the world (our amazing human eternal soul)..
The Eleventh Wonder of the World (our amazing human eternal heart).
The Twelfth Wonder of the world (our amazing human eternal spirit).
Coming soon:
The Thirteenth Wonder of the world (our amazing journey thereafter).

 JERRY RHOADS PUBLISHING 2024

www.ingramcontent.com/pod-product-compliance
Lightning Source LLC
Chambersburg PA
CBHW052129030426
42337CB00028B/5089